THE
PROBLEM
HORSE

by

Reginald S. Summerhays

Illustrations by

John Board

Published by
Melvin Powers
WILSHIRE BOOK COMPANY
12015 Sherman Road
No. Hollywood, California 91605
Telephone: (213) 875-1711 / (818) 983-1105

Published in the United States 1960
by A. S. BARNES AND COMPANY, INC., NEW YORK

Copyright © 1959 by J. A. Allen and Company

Library of Congress Catalog Card Number: 60-11687

Printed by

HAL LEIGHTON PRINTING COMPANY
P.O. Box 3952
North Hollywood, California 91605
Telephone: (818) 983-1105

ISBN 0-87980-200-6

Printed in the United States of America

CONTENTS

ILLUSTRATIONS

Preface

BEFORE asking you to read this book I would put one question to you. Have you ever owned a perfectly mannered horse? If you have, you will realize how great is the gulf between him and the other fellow who is not *quite* all he should be. If you have not, a pleasant surprise awaits you.

Foals, like infants, present themselves to the world entirely innocent and free from all the little faults and failings so many of which make the adult not easily recognizable as the successor to the hour-old wonder. That, at any rate, is what we are told, and it is probably strictly true. It is, however, sure enough that the young thing may inherit some of its parents' tendencies, whether for good or otherwise ; and therein lies much of the trouble with which those who have the care and handling of horses have to deal. If we knew whether the trouble was hereditary or not, its cure would be the easier.

Now it seems to me to be remarkable that there are over two dozen vices or failings to be found in horses in general. In particular, and most unhappily, one or more are to be found in very many horses. I believe all with but two or three exceptions to be curable, or to be such that they can be dealt with confidently and with satisfactory results by the person in charge whether mounted or on foot. This is a bold statement to make but it is true.

I first realized how widespread are these deviations from the straight and true equine path when, as editor of *Riding*, it occurred to me that I must have received perhaps thousands of letters, each telling me that this or that other-

7

wise perfect horse *would* do this or declined to do that, and asking what was the cure. In the greater number of cases there are probably several cures or remedies for each trouble ; the more knowledgeable the horseman, the more cures he will find and the less he may look with favour upon my remedies, many of which can truly be called ' home-made ', being the result of practical experience.

Out of a mass of tricks and dodges I have picked a remedy or two for each trouble—remedies that I know to be practical, effective, and foolproof as far as anything can be foolproof. I believe this to be better for the novice, or the not very experienced horseman for whom I have written this book, than to suggest that he should try so and so and, if that does not work, that he might find such and such effective. It is perhaps better, too, than to say that this person recommends one way to tackle the job while another expert believes in something quite different. Feeling like one who is shouting his wares for sale, I must add that no expensive apparatus is required for any of my cures, and that they are entirely harmless—at least I sincerely hope so, but many horses are uncertain creatures.

Let me say this, however—when considering any form of vice or misbehaviour, always regard the possibility that the horse has something organically wrong with him which may be the cause of the trouble. If you are in doubt, or the trouble is particularly baffling, consult your veterinary surgeon, and be satisfied only after a complete overhaul of all the organs.

Well, having opened such a happy vista for owners who would have their just-not-quite perfect horse transformed into the same blameless animal which it was when it was foaled, let me say with conviction and great sincerity that, although many horses are predisposed to waywardness

8

through inherited flighty or wilful tendencies, nearly every vice or misbehaviour is the result of the thoughtlessness, stupidity, or active or passive cruelty of man. A horse does something wrong, and man, the master, shows him he is wrong and what he wants him to do. That is just what *should* happen, but hardly ever does the man realize that why the horse did wrong was *because he did not understand.* He forgets, or does not know, that in nearly everything the horse's mind works extraordinarily slowly, and that a horse may, in order to understand simple things, require to be shown a dozen times. It does not follow at all that the man may be rough or even cruel in his methods of putting the horse right, but, as likely as not, he does not do it in a way which restores the horse's confidence the least little bit ; probably he just repeats the same aid, which the horse did not understand, or misunderstood, before.

Neither horse nor man is therefore helped, tempers get frayed, and the horse loses still more of that confidence in man without which he is a bewildered, and, in consequence, an unhappy animal. Remember always that, just as having nothing to do turns nice children into little pests, so too much food and not enough work is the cause of much of the trouble in the horses with which I am dealing and, by the way, causes unnecessary vet's bills to be incurred. Never wrap a horse in cottonwool as so many people do who own horses for their own pleasure. If all horses were given plenty of good food and lots of work, some of these chapters would not need to be written. It is such sins of omission and commission which create that unnecessary, always irritating, and sometimes dangerous animal, The Problem Horse.

Perhaps a few last words are appropriate to this Preface. Many who read this book may say that some of the suggestions I have made are not in keeping with modern practice, that cures, for instance, can be found more in the entire reschooling of the horse. Substantially I would agree with this, but who in these days has the time or a reliable groom who can be trusted to take a horse into a paddock and there quietly work on him day after day for perhaps two or three months? This is an age when the great majority of owners do their own horses. I have, in writing this, had in mind the many occasions when a rider meets trouble and has to cope with it *on the instant,* rough and ready though the method may be. I know the value of this for I have ridden scores and scores of ill-trained, vicious, half-broken horses and many of the greenest of the green : in the army, when buying remounts in the 1914 war, and young horses from Ireland, often not much more than halter-broken. I've met them all; the rearers, the kickers, the jibbers, the biters, the runaways and a couple of madmen; it's always then a case of who's to be master. No holds can be barred then. The whole basis of the relationship of horse and man is that man must be the master.

R. S. SUMMERHAYS

1. *Hard to Mount*

ALL forms of misbehaviour in horses can be cured—or
at least for safety's sake I had better say ' nearly all '.
Which, I wonder, of the many irritating habits is the most
annoying ? The horse which will not stand to be mounted,
the animal which keeps you struggling for five minutes
before you can get his bridle on, or the so-called courageous
fellow which, after a day's hunting, will jog every step of the
way home ? Each is more exasperating than the last, and
all the application of patience—that golden key to success
which all horsemen are supposed to carry with them—
seems of little avail.

Let us take the first trouble. Here, I think, is a cast-
iron remedy. Why will many horses not stand to be
mounted ? Well, why *should* they, when we consider that
they know they are about to be mounted and ridden off, and
the natural thing is to move at once ? More than this, the
mounting business to a horse must be a not too pleasant
operation. Notice the way the average person gets into the
saddle. The reins are, as likely as not, held unevenly and
too tight, and often the mouth is jerked in the process.
To add to these little inconveniences, the rider's toe may
well be stuck in pretty hard just behind the girth, and at the
same time the saddle may be wrenched over the back a
couple of inches or so out of the true, pulling the girths
round at the same time. No wonder the horse puts up a
protest in the form of moving off in the hope of walking
away from these nuisances.

Now then for the remedy, which I have found has not
failed and which you may try with confidence.

For the first few times you need an assistant, who should stand in front of your horse without holding his bridle. He may lay his hand on your horse's nose if the latter seems likely to move on. At the very moment when you mount, this assistant should give your horse a piece of sugar, a slice of carrot or apple, or anything which the horse particularly fancies. It is as well to dismount and repeat this once or twice, but no more. For the next two or three days you should continue to use your assistant in the same way, in order to get your horse well accustomed to expect something good while he stands still ; after which your assistant should stand on the *near* side against the horse's shoulder, and at the moment of your mounting should feed him from there in such a way that he has to turn his head well round to get what is offered. This should be repeated as I have just described for a day or so, after which this assistance can be dispensed with.

When you now come to mount alone you should let your horse take a smell at your left hand, so that he may know that you have in it what he has now come to look for ; you should then mount quickly, and the moment you are in the saddle give him his reward. You will find he will swing his head round to receive it without moving off. Of course, it would be rather ridiculous to have to bribe your horse in this way every time you mount for the rest of your riding days on this particular horse, and it is quite unnecessary to do so. You should, however, let him have a bit of something good from time to time from your position in the saddle, especially if he shows a tendency to fall from grace. In other words, you should check in time any inclination on his part to move off before you decide that it is time to set out on your ride.

To make this cure (which I recommend to you with

' *He should give him anything the horse particularly fancies.*'

13

confidence) of a permanent character, it will be obvious that you should be as quiet in your mounting as you well can be.

Good things offered from the hand are all very nice, but you can hardly expect a horse, however much he may relish them, to undergo the discomforts which may be inflicted upon him without putting up some form of movement as protest. If you are sensible enough to mount from a mounting-block, the whole proceeding is simplified, as there will be so much less disturbance to the horse. It may be found, however, when you are mounting from the mounting-block without assistance, that the horse in turning his head to you swings out his quarters, making mounting difficult. You should therefore see that your assistant operates from the off-side shoulder, which will keep the quarters in ; and all you have to do when mounting alone is to feed him, the moment you are in the saddle, from your right hand or off-side.

2. *Hard to Bridle*

AT the best of times, it is not very pleasant to see a horse having a bridle put on him. This is particularly so when a small man is getting a sixteen-hand horse ready. It is mostly, even with a tractable horse, an affair of standing on the tip of the toes and stretching the arms to an uncomfortable extent ; and with an unruly animal the bridle usually gets pushed all over the horse's face.

Can you wonder that the average horse is difficult to bridle, and can you wonder that most riders suffer anything from annoyance to exasperation when they put a bridle on a horse's head ? The struggling and straining on tiptoe suffered by most is only too well known, and for the short-legged rider it often becomes a real physical effort. Let us look at it from the horse's point of view, for to him the process of being bridled is perhaps the worst feature of the day's routine. He has literally a handful of metal pushed into his mouth, and more often than not the bridle cheek-straps on either side are drawn roughly over his eyelids, and both ears are flattened. No wonder he resents it, no wonder he raises his head higher and higher, to the increasing annoyance of the man who is putting on his tack.

Any horse, however, can be taught to help rather than to hinder if he is approached in the proper way. First let us repeat what is probably known to all—the right way to bridle a horse. Undo the throat-lash, the nose-band and the curb-chain. Slip the head of the bridle over the left arm with the brow-band and nose-band facing your body, and with the right hand draw the reins over the horse's neck and place them on the withers. Then with the right hand take the top of the bridle and draw it up over the horse's head. Keep the bit in the left hand and place it between the horse's teeth, if necessary opening the side of the mouth with thumb and forefinger, and ease the bit into position.

The way to handle a horse which is difficult to bridle is to turn his head away from the manger to the door, mount a low stool, which should be placed on his near side, and then gently and with great care do as I have just described, placing the right wrist and forearm along the top of his neck up to his poll as the bridle is being drawn up firmly, but not too firmly, over his poll. The object in getting on a stool is to be able to bring a certain amount of pressure to keep the head low, and, more important than this, to be able to see in the process that the bridle is drawn up in such a way that the eyes are not rubbed by any portion of the leather as the bridle is drawn into position, nor the ears unduly pushed and pulled about.

The horse raises his head only as a defensive measure against the inconvenience which he knows he will suffer in the ordinary way ; and if the eyes are kept clear, and the bit placed in the mouth in such a way that the lips are not pinched, he will in a very short space of time realize that this bridling process is something not so very unpleasant after all.

The object in doing this from a stool is obviously to give better control all round and save the rider from stretching and straining on tiptoe. It will be unnecessary, of course, to have a stool for a tall man putting a bridle on a reasonably small horse, or for any person doing the same on a small pony, but the wrist and forearm should always be placed on the horse's head if he is at all liable to resent being bridled.

After using this method a few times on any ordinary horse it should be quite unnecessary to make use of a stool, unless, of course, the horse is particularly temperamental ; and I recommend that the horse should on each occasion be rewarded for good behaviour. Remember that he does not resent having the bridle put on merely because it is a bridle, but solely on account of the inconvenience and sometimes real pain which is caused.

A well-behaved horse will lower his head and give every assistance in having his bridle put on, but only those horses will do this who know that in the process they will be put to the minimum amount of inconvenience. You will find if you follow these instructions that, in but a short space of time, the well-known struggles will cease and bridling will become a pleasure rather than what it is so often—quite a nuisance.

3. *Water-shy*

It is a curious thing how many admirably behaved horses, that will go anywhere and do anything, fight shy of water. I do not necessarily mean horses that will not go over water when hounds are running, but horses that simply will not walk through streams. How many people, I wonder, while taking a pleasant hack come to a small stream or water-splash on a road and find it just impossible to get their horse through it? You cannot pull a horse where it does not want to go, and certainly no one wants to stand in the middle of a stream and try to persuade a horse to join him and follow him through it.

I suppose one needs to go back to the history of these things to find out why a horse objects to water in this form. If we could find the root cause then perhaps the cure would be easier. Actually there is a cure, and a simple one, though it requires, like most other forms of training for horses, a certain amount of patience.

All that is required, in addition to plenty of patience, is a pair of gum-boots ; but the whole business will be made much easier if you can find a companion who has a horse which does not mind going through water or standing in water. You need to carry with you, too, some sugar or slices of carrot. Take your horse, then, to the water and stand in the stream in your gum-boots. You want to make it clear to him that there is nothing to fear. Do not attempt to pull him into the water. Stand in the water and idly kick it about, your idea being to get some water on to his legs as unostentatiously as possible. Of course if you have a friend whose horse is standing in the water it will help to

18

'*Make it clear to him that there is nothing to fear.*'

19

make the whole thing appear to your horse less fearsome, and really quite natural.

After you have done this for a short while move round him and get him as close as you can to the water without in any way forcing him, bringing his quarters more to the water than his forehand. As I have said, you cannot pull a horse into water if he does not want to go, but with a little judicious petting and by making a bit of a fuss of him you can very often edge his quarters to the water.

You will find in the course of time—and it may be quite soon—that he will get so far in that his fetlocks are covered with water, and when you have succeeded in doing this the battle is more than half won.

You should, of course, from the outset have the reins over his head, and during the period I have described you should keep up contact with the other horse, splashing the water about in a quiet way all the time. Actually horses like water. I think they like the sound of it and the feel of it, and when you have got them over the initial stage of getting used to it, the rest you will find is easy enough. You must, however, take great care not to force this process upon your horse ; for, if he thinks he is being made to do something, he will certainly try to back out, in the literal sense.

If your first attempt to teach your horse to become accustomed to water does not meet with complete success, as may very well be the case, do not over-press him, but give up the job for the time being and take him there again on the next possible occasion. It is worth taking some trouble because it is most exasperating to be in company and come across a water-splash or stream and to find that the party has to go on and leave you behind, or return with you and so perhaps spoil a good ride. How many people,

I wonder, have had a good hunt spoilt, say with the Devon and Somerset, when they have found their horses refuse to go through one of the numerous fords on the Barle or Exe ? Yet, by the way, how obviously horses enjoy going through good deep water, if they have not this really annoying habit of being water-shy. How good it is to jump a water-filled ditch, a dyke on a marsh, or some such obstacle, when you know that your horse will take water in his stride just as a good hunter will face up to any ordinary hunting obstacle.

4. *Bad Stable Manners*

SOME ordinarily well-behaved and altogether attractive horses are quite offensive in the stable. Instead of acting consistently with their outdoor behaviour they will lay back their ears, raise a hind leg in a menacing fashion, and possibly show the whites of their eyes. It may mean nothing, though it is hardly the welcome one would wish for, but it may well mean that they are really nasty customers and have to be watched if trouble is to be avoided.

It is difficult to trace the cause of many bad habits in horses, but you may be fairly certain that horses which show signs such as these have been in their early days subjected, if not to some form of cruelty, to rough behaviour of some description. This may not have amounted to more than impatient handling and an unnecessary amount of noise produced either by the voice or by the clattering of pails and brooms and pitchforks more or less thrown about. Horses are particularly sensitive to noise.

It may be, too, that the particular horse has a very sensitive skin. Many grooms seem to disregard this altogether, grooming a horse with a skin of this sort with as

'*Some ordinarily well-behaved horses are quite offensive in the stable.*'

much vigour as if he had the hide of a rhinoceros. A thin-skinned horse should be groomed with the softest brush or rubber, or even with the hand alone. To disregard a horse's feelings in this way leads to his biting and kicking, and he will in a very short time associate anyone coming into the stable with one or other of the things he dislikes, as I have described. There are, too, horses that are really vicious, that will kick out at you or bite and behave in a way that is frankly dangerous. Fortunately, such horses are few and far between. The method of overcoming these ills in horses, from the mild to the vicious, is simple, although somewhat laborious and takes a considerable amount of time.

You must bring your horse to understand that your presence in the stable is something not only not to be feared but also rather to be looked forward to ; so make up your mind to spend some time each day to this end. Take a stool out of the harness room and sit on it in his box. Read, knit, or keep yourself occupied in some way and just sit there for as long as you can spare each day. You can have some slices of apple or carrot or what you will, and after a while just hold out a bit to him. Do not walk up to him, or make a fuss of him, or handle him ; just, as it were, go in, sit down, and go out again. Results will of course depend upon the temperament of the horse, but you can be as near certain of this as of anything, that in course of time he will not give any more unwelcome displays either to you or to anyone else. Knowing his temperamental nature it is wiser, at any rate while he is being gentled in this way, to warn any stranger coming into the box to be as quiet as possible and not to go up to him straight away.

What I have suggested above as a cure is not so easy when your horse is kept in a stall, owing to the much more confined space ; about all you can do then is to sit on the manger and dangle your legs. The idea, after all, is the same : you must make him think of your presence as something soothing and rather to be looked forward to than otherwise.

If you ' do ' your own horse, as so many have to in these days, the probability is that misbehaviour of this sort will be a very mild affair ; but if the strapping is done by a groom I should take particular care to notice whether he is unduly rough.

I have known cases of really vicious horses being cured by this method, so you may have every hope that if your horse is a bit white-eyed in the stable, a bit twitchy about the tail, and shows a suspicious raising of a hind leg, a cure will be effected eventually.

5. *Unwilling to Walk*

JUST as drops of water wear away stone, so a jig-jogging horse wears away his constitution—and much more quickly. Few people seem to realize how harmful this always-up-on-his-toes business is to a horse, and in consequence few people seem to take the trouble to correct it. Perhaps it is because to do so is a tiring job.

I think people react to this vice in four different ways. First there are those who do not react at all ! They just leave the thing where it is. Then we have those who do make an attempt to steady their horses down to a walk, but who, on finding that doing this for half a dozen paces is no good at all, seem to give up the job as not worthwhile or too fatiguing. We have too the type of person who rather enjoys sitting on a horse which is ' tittuping ' along when it

'A device to soothe the nervy horse.'

should be walking ; and there is no doubt that many horses are very comfortable at this—I was going to say 'gait', but actually it is no gait at all. On the other hand, some horses are extremely uncomfortable! The fourth class is the worst, and consists of those who consider that they look very nice, and who perhaps hope they are stamped in the minds of onlookers as real horsemen as they prance gaily down the street.

Various methods have been put forward for curing this trouble in horses, which has its roots in temperament. Many horses become excited when they set out from the stable. Many become even more excited after the first trot, and after a canter or gallop the last thing apparently they will do is to settle down when asked to walk.

Now, the cures I have for this vice require much patience. You must just *make* your horse walk, but first do not, as many people do, sit tight in the saddle. This only serves to make your horse get tense and still more up on his toes. Adjust your reins to the right length, sit loosely in the saddle, and proceed to walk. Directly he shows signs of 'breaking' draw your horse's head in quietly and steadily till he drops into a walk again, and then slacken the reins once more. He will 'break' again at once, and you must repeat the procedure—and go on doing this with a soothing word here and there. It is your will against his, and if you persevere you will be certain to succeed. Your horse does not want to jig-jog ; he does it only because he is over-excited, and you must just calm him down, remembering all the time to sit loosely, soothe him quietly, and never in any circumstances show any form of impatience or irritation either by word or in rein action.

Either as an alternative or as an additional aid, take the reins in one hand, and with the fingers of the other pull up a bit of your horse's skin at the top of the shoulders and 'play' with it. This is an old dodge often applied for many different reasons. It has the effect of taking the horse's mind off something which up to then has been uppermost in his mind, and is often most effective in this matter of the jig-jog.

One other device to soothe the nervy horse : sit just a little farther forward in your saddle, put your first and second fingers on either side of his neck, and from the poll to the wither draw them slowly down, repeating the dose as required. This, as with the other cures, to be taken with the addition of an appropriately soothing and comforting voice.

You will probably meet with a good measure of success on your first attempt to right this fault. The extent of this will depend largely on the temperament of your horse and whether he has been hard-galloped or just lightly cantered on the ride ; but most of all it will depend upon your implacable will to succeed. Remember that a horse is tremendously influenced by its rider's mentality. I have heard it said that it is an indication of horsemanship to be able to make a horse walk which is unwilling to do so, and although this is rather a sweeping statement there is much truth in it.

You have probably heard people discussing a day's hunting and how gallantly their horses carried them ; and to illustrate a horse's courage and stamina they will describe how he came back ' all the way to the stables up on his toes '. This is neither courage nor stamina—it is just over-excitability, and has the worst possible effect upon the horse. If the person concerned had said how well he had been carried throughout the day and that he had tried his utmost to make his horse walk on the way back with only

partial success, he would appear in the eyes of the knowledgeable a real horseman rather than a very unthoughtful and
boastful one. Returning from hunting is not perhaps the
best time to try to cure your horse of the vice of jig-jogging,
but while you are on his back you should try even more
assiduously than when out hacking. By the way, after
hunting be sure to dismount and walk at his side as much
as you can. This will help to soothe him.

6. *Pulling*

ONE of the worst of all vices, and the one with the
greatest number of cures or so-called cures, is pulling.
Horses pull for so many reasons : natural excitability,
too many measures of corn, an unsympathetic rider
on top, bad hands on the reins, or an uncomfortable
bit in the mouth or saddle on the back. People think that
a horse is extremely stupid to pull because in doing so he
merely accentuates the amount of pulling that goes on from
his rider and so increases his own discomfort. This is true,
but his stupidity is not so great as you would think. In fact
there is quite a lot of sound sense in it. A horse pulls on the
principle that it is a way out of his trouble, and he hopes by
his superior strength to defeat you in the battle—and at times
he does. If you start to run away from me and I catch you by
the tail of your coat and pull against you, you will pull against
me in the hope of getting free, and that is very much what a
horse does.

In this chapter I am not attempting to show you the
many things that can be done to prevent a horse from
pulling, the different bits that can be tried to improve the
state of affairs, the sympathetic touch on the reins, the

give-and-take and so on, for the cure is a mixture of these things and of many others as well. What I am dealing with now is the way to stop a puller. Everybody should be equipped with a safety device about his person, and I will give you one to carry just in case you find yourself up on a bad puller.

The more a person rides the more he wishes to ride different horses. This is most commendable and enjoyable and is the only way in which real horsemen are made. The more horses you ride the more likely you are to come up against a real puller. I must assume that you have applied what methods you have been taught to check your horse whose pace is increasing until you have arrived at the stage where you just cannot hold him any longer and he has obtained complete control.

The best way of stopping a horse which is in this state is to shorten your reins, get hold of his head good and strong, and bring your left rein over his neck just about a hand's length in front of his withers. Simultaneously with this movement place your right hand as low down his neck on the off-side as possible and hold him hard from that position. The near-side rein, therefore, is over his neck, the off-side rein is held as low as possible, and if you do this I shall be surprised if you do not pull him up. This is the method taught to lads in racing stables ; goodness knows they have to ride pullers, and it is certain that, at their age and with their physique, brute force alone will not carry them very far when it comes to straight pulling on a horse's mouth.

Another method which I find effective, although it is certainly a rough-and-ready method, is to shorten your reins, stand up in your stirrups, get your knees into the saddle as hard as you can and drop your reins to him.

'Get your knees into the saddle as hard as you can and drop your reins to him.'

Then pull on them with a strong and steady pull and drop them again, repeating this two or three times. With luck your horse will begin to be puzzled at this method and to wonder quite what he is going to do about it, and he may stop after the third or fourth pull. If this fails it looks as if you are really up against it ; and I have then found it very effective if you get your hands as high up his neck as possible and lift his head into the air, and then drop your hands to him and repeat the dose again. Two or three applications of this method following the one described immediately before should do the trick. I recommend the first method in preference. As a rather grim ending to this paragraph, how often we read in the papers of runaway horses causing fatal injury to the rider or serious damage. We may be sure the unfortunate person had never been *taught* how to stop a runaway. All riders should bear this in mind most seriously.

So many people encourage horses to pull. They like to go for a good gallop—but they go at an uncollected gallop, and this teaches a horse to become a puller. It is surprising how many people who are riding a puller say, ' I gave him a good gallop to take it out of him.' This is absurd because, in a sense, the more you gallop a horse the less you take it out of him ; a horse that is galloped for this purpose will become more and more the confirmed puller, which is surely one of the big nuisances in the horse world.

7. *Stable-banging and -kicking*

AMONG stable vices we must include banging on the half-door of the box. Some people, who are given to attributing all sorts of signs and wonders found in horses to their great intelligence, think this is a sensible and attractive

35

way in which the horse calls for his food. To some extent
this is true, for the horse will put his head over the half-door
and paw the ground and bang on the door with his knees.
This I think is particularly so with stallions, which perhaps
shows that it is more an inclination to leave the box than a
call for food. Whatever the reason, the fact remains that
this often leads to 'big' knees; and the swelling is quite
difficult to reduce, especially if it is neglected.

An obvious way of avoiding the damage is to pad the
door with sacking stuffed with straw, or any tough material
as a covering with any soft material as packing. This,
however, is not entirely satisfactory, because sooner or later
—and it is generally sooner—the horse will tear or wear a
hole in the material; and once that comes about the
deterioration is pretty fast.

There is a device which, I think, is a complete answer,
and it can be easily erected. Set back from the half-door
and attached to two strong hinges, at about the height of
the horse's chest, is placed a board which in depth just about
covers the chest. At one end, therefore, you have hinges to
enable the board to be opened like a door, and at the other
end you have some bolt or latch which is fastened just as any
door is fastened to shut it tight. The effect is obvious;
the horse cannot put his head over the half-door and bang
his knees, yet he can put his head over the plank and he can
paw to his heart's content—but his knees will not reach the
half-door. The only possible inconvenience is that you
either have to open what in effect is two doors, or you
open one and stoop under the other to reach the horse. I
think in any event it is a good idea, especially if the horse is
a show animal and would be at a disadvantage in the ring
with a big knee.

Another remedy is to buckle a strap—something similar to

a dog collar—above the knee, attach a stout cord to one side of the collar and thread it through a small round block of wood, attaching the other end of the cord to the collar on the opposite side of the knee. In other words, you have hung on the front of the cannon-bone a round block of wood which taps the horse on each and every occasion when he raises his knee to start banging. He will not like this, and you will probably find that he will not only give up banging on the door but will also cease this pawing of the stable floor which is wearing not only to his shoes but also to his temperament.

Many horses, as we know, when tied up in their stalls will kick at the side. The fact that it must give them a certain amount of pain and that it is more often than not productive of lumps and bumps seems to have very little effect, and they just go on doing it. The method I have described above for door-banging may not be possible in the case of a kicker, because while you may put an attachment to a horse's forelegs without much fear of the horse making trouble, to fix something to his hind legs is another business altogether, and most horses wouldn't stand it for a moment. If your horse is placid, however, you can try it ; the fitment should be just above the fetlock joint so that the block of wood rests on the coronet.

A more satisfactory cure perhaps, as it entails less risk, is to tie a sack against the supporting post of the stall division and tie round it or fix on it in some way some branches from gorse bushes. Horses, as we know, are very shy of gorse—you will certainly have noticed this if you ride through gorse bushes—and a horse is not likely to kick long against anything of that sort. Care must be taken during the cure to see that none of the gorse spikes have embedded themselves in the leg. If they have they are likely to set up a certain amount of inflammation.

Although I have put these two vices together in one chapter the causes of the two are different. In the first, no doubt the banging is the result of a perfectly natural excitement when feed-time is drawing near—an anxious anticipation of good things—but the second, this kicking at the only obstruction that is available, is a vice which may arise from a number of causes. It may be some irritation in the foot or leg. It is believed by many that, whatever may be the cause, a horse derives quite an amount of satisfaction from hearing the repeated bangs. This may be so, and anyway the fact remains that a horse will keep it up for a long while to the great irritation of those, human or equine, who may be within reach of the sound. In any event these are bad stable habits, and all horsemen should do their best to stop them as soon as possible. Like all bad habits the longer they are left the more difficult they are to cure.

8. *Bucking*

To the inexperienced a bucking horse can be a real terror, but to the well-experienced it does not cause much anxiety. Indeed, many riders rather enjoy a buck or two when they first get on the turf as perhaps a sign of light-hearted gaiety which can well be shared with the horse. However that may be, bucking, from whatever cause, is a thing to put an end to, and the sooner the better.

Probably the most common cause of bucking has its root in the old trouble, under-work and over-feeding ; and if this is so it is just a piece of light-hearted devilment. It may arise, too, and often does, through a cold saddle lying on a very sensitive part of a horse, or from the girths having

' You are well and truly flung off.'

been hitched up too tight or pinching the flesh. Again, it may be that the horse is really resentful of control, and bucking presents itself to him as being one of the ready means of getting rid of his rider. In this case he may well be not a bad judge. There are other means, of course : rolling, rearing, and finding a convenient wall to bang a rider's leg against—a most unpleasant business and fortunately very rarely encountered, but, I can assure you that, when met with, it leaves a rider feeling pretty helpless.

There is one good thing to be said about bucking, and it is that a horse usually gives fair warning of what he intends to do. First he will generally buck either almost directly after he has been mounted or when he gets to a place such as a stretch of turf where he expects to be asked to canter. Many horses, too, will fling two or three good ones when hounds start to run. Wherever or whenever it may be, a horse, as I say, usually gives some warning ; you can feel his back getting up, his head getting down ; these are two things he must do and without which he cannot buck.

Now it seems obvious to me, and you must surely agree, that the thing to do is to keep your horse's head up ; and if you keep his head up you will help to keep his back down. And just in case you cannot keep his back down you must get your seat away from the saddle, by doing which you will avoid being flung on his neck or more probably through the air. Directly, therefore, you feel that your horse is about to start bucking, clap your knees hard in, get out of the saddle and reasonably far forward, and with your reins short get hold of his head and lift it up with a sharp one or two on his mouth, all this with lightning speed. It is a wise thing to treat him rough with your voice.

When riding a determined bucker you will understand

that a good deal of resolution is required, and it is not to be expected that at the first buck you will be successful ; you must therefore, if he continues, keep on at him in the same way and sit, or rather grip with your knees, just as hard as you possibly can. It is wise, and indeed essential, that when riding a horse with this vice you should pass the end of one rein through one hand into the other hand, thus forming a bridge which prevents him from stretching out his head to lengthen the reins. If the reins do get pulled through your hands, it is more likely than not that you will be finished, or rather shot in the air, because you will lose control of his head and go back on the saddle, and he will see that by arching his back, which is part of the process of bucking, you are well and truly flung off.

Personally, *immediately* after a bucking bout, I always hit a horse a couple of good ones down the shoulder, and I do this because even though he may have bucked through sheer light-heartedness it is not for him to decide what he will do and what he will not do, and bucking, if unchecked, can well develop into an unpleasant and dangerous trick.

9. *Shying*

JUST as bucking is so often the result of under-working and over-feeding, so too is shying. So too in fact are probably the majority of vices, in the stable and out of it. Shying, however, may be the result of a real nervous temperament, a defect in vision, or a strong dislike arising originally perhaps through fear of some particular object or, indeed, of some thing highly coloured.

It is my belief that many horses do not become shyers through any of the above causes but are literally invited to

'And then, of course, the fun begins.'

44

become so by inexperienced or, more likely, really nervous riders. One can hardly pick up a book on horses or horsemanship without reading how greatly a horse is affected by the mentality of its rider, and there is nothing truer in horsemanship than this. It follows, therefore, that many horses are quite unwittingly and unconsciously taught to shy by their riders. How often does a rider coming round a bend in the road see a steam-roller, or something perhaps less fearsome, and at once ' gets hold ' of his horse, tightens the seat and tightens the hold on the reins, and likely enough on the horse's mouth. The horse naturally thinks ' Gosh, what's this coming along ? Evidently something pretty fearful. We must *both* look out.' And then, of course, the fun begins ; he will whip round, refuse to advance, or approach crab-fashion and take you towards a path, a ditch, or hedge, or all three of them ; a very unpleasant and disturbing business.

The cure for this sort of thing is fairly obvious and is founded entirely on commonsense. When approaching the object likely to cause the trouble do just the reverse of what I have explained above as being likely to take place. Let your touch on the reins be very light, take very little hold of your horse's mouth and let your seat be literally a relaxed one. If you are one of those who adopt the good practice of talking to your horse, then do a bit of talking in the most soothing voice you can command and do everything you can to make the horse feel that the last thing he and you need worry about is the approaching object.

Many people recommend turning a horse this way or turning him that, catching hold of his head and driving him on ; but these are not cures, they are merely methods, adopted no doubt on many occasions very successfully, to get the horse past the object. But if you follow them you will have the same trouble in the future and probably to an increasing extent.

There are horses, of course, which find imaginary birds in hedges and make a rare to-do about it, and as the shying then is always sudden and sometimes accompanied by a considerable swerving to the off my opinion is that such should be corrected. There is the inconsiderate old lady, and other people of all ages and both sexes, who will open an umbrella under a horse's nose. I have had this done to me a number of times, which really seems extraordinary ; and no one can be surprised if a horse shies in such circumstances. This being a shy from pure fright and one which really cannot be anticipated there is no cure, and it must be suffered and the horse soothed.

It is a curious thing how seldom horses will shy while out hunting ; indeed I have the impression that they never do, or at any rate that such a thing is most rare ; they will buck and they will rear but they will not shy. Does this mean that ordinary shying is very largely the result of a mental process and that a horse, when hounds are running or when he is with hounds, has his mind so concentrated that the fear of objects somewhat out of the normal does not come into his mind ? I am not very certain about this and I should like to hear what knowledgeable horsemen have to say about it. Whenever it is believed that shying is the result of fear, opportunity should be found to overcome this. I remember that a woman once wrote to me that she had the most darling horse in the world—perfect in every way except that it was petrified on encountering pigs ; and could I help her ? I replied, ' Introduce your horse to pigs and let them become well acquainted.' Two weeks later she wrote that it was the perfect cure. This shying is often just as simple as all that.

10. *Rearing, Jibbing, and the Nappy Horse*

WITH the rearer I include the jibbing horse and the nappy one. All horses that have these vices are hard to give away, let alone to sell. It is curious, by the way, that a man of very considerable experience, the manager of a big riding stable, told me that the more *inexperienced* the rider the better a nappy horse went under him, and conversely the more experienced the rider the more the nappy horse played up. His theory was that nappiness is a form of rebellion against authority, and, as the inexperienced rider does not pretend to have much authority, a horse ridden by him is quite content to take the ride more or less according to his own ideas and come back again without any trouble. If, however, the horse has an experienced rider on board he just fights against the authority which is, of course, at once applied. This is interesting, and I believe there is a good deal of truth in it, but the point we have now to decide is how we may deal successfully with these three vices.

Much has been written and many cures have been advanced, but I will tell you what I think will be most likely to get you out of your immediate trouble. Rearing if deliberate or vicious is a real vice and a dangerous one. Never mind what the cause is—if you can't cure it you may just as well have the horse destroyed before he smashes you up. Fortunately a horse that rears rarely goes over backward, unless pulled back by the rider, and usually the first rear is less pronounced than those that follow. The last thing you must do, of course, is to pull on the horse's mouth, or you may well pull him over backward. Although it looks a most skilful proceeding to be able to sit on a horse that is doing a good rear, if the knee grip is good, there is very little to it.   You must just ease his head and sit as far forward as you can.   The point, however, is, when he comes to the ground, and *immediately* he touches the ground, to have a strong pull on one rein so that he comes round in a circle, and to kick him with your heel on the side that you are pulling.   Keep this up vigorously and continuously, and if you can get him round three or four or even more times you will find that the action has been so bewildering to him that he is most unlikely to rear again.

Do not pause, however, when the circling is complete, but drive him on with your heels and voice and, if this is ineffective, with your stick.   What you have done really is to confuse his mind, and by these rapid circles you have attained a certain mastery over the horse.   It is for you to press him back to the job of work he was required to do, with such determination and such speed that he has no time to think twice.

Fortunately few but experienced riders are asked to ride rearers and few experienced ones will ride them if they know what the trouble is ; but you and those not so knowledgeable in horsemanship may well be asked to ride jibbers and nappy horses.   Indeed if you are in the habit of hiring a horse and riding alone from stables you will very often find you are riding a nappy or semi-nappy horse, because school horses do the greater part of their riding in company and, the herd instinct being very strong in horses, they get to dislike going out alone.

Again there are many cures or so-called cures for these horses and for jibbers, but my belief is that the most practical cure is really a repetition of what I have written in regard to the rearing horse—mastery through bewilderment and

If the knee grip is good, there is very little to it.'

through the most inflexible determination which you can produce to make the horse get on with the allotted job. A jibber, besides refusing to go forward will often run backward, and a nappy horse will swing round in either direction and refuse to go forward. Well, if space permits, not only let him run back but *make* him run back, and if you can bang his quarters into a wall, a hedge or a fence you have found quite an effective aid to your cure. If he does not go forward then, turn him round, and do not forget to use your heel good and hard and to liven things up a bit with your stick. With a nappy horse apply the circling movement with strength of leg and strength of will.

11. *Crib-biting, Wind-sucking, and Weaving*

THESE are most offensive habits and undoubtedly the worst of stable vices. Crib-biting is quite a common trouble, more so perhaps than weaving, and to my mind it is a more unpleasant habit to see in a horse and certainly more detrimental to its health.

Cribbing, as you probably know, is when a horse takes its manger or any other suitable projection in its teeth and appears to tear at it, making disagreeable sucking noises the while. Doing this wears down a horse's teeth, making them appear somewhat like the bevelling of a chisel. That is comparatively innoxious, but I mention it because an easy though not infallible way of telling a cribber when he is not within reach of anything to crib is to part his lips and look for the bevelling. I should say that cribbers' digestive organs become almost invariably upset, and chronically so ; and you rarely see them with much flesh upon them. I have, however, come across lifelong crib-biters which are apparently none the worse for this vice — and that is curious.

Wind-sucking usually follows and is the result of crib-biting. The horse raises his head and sucks in wind—a most unpleasant proceeding and one very harmful to his condition.

Weaving is a most curious and wearing habit in horses, consisting of waving the head endlessly from side to side pendulum-fashion, at the same time shifting the weight from forefoot to forefoot rather in the manner of the stage policeman.

A preventative—a cure can hardly be found—is to suspend two cords, with a brick at the end of each, over the half-door of the loose-box in such a way that the horse when looking out of the box places his head between them. When weaving, he will cause the two bricks to swing from side to side ; the resultant irritation, disturbance and confusion will cause him to cease weaving.

Another method of stopping a horse weaving is to tie his head on either side, pillar-chain fashion.

There are a dozen and more alleged cures for crib-biters, wind-suckers, and weavers ; but they are really incurable. An effective way to stop the sort of sucking which results from the crib-biting is to put a special form of wind-sucking strap round the horse's neck just where it joins the head. Some of the other methods suggested are not very practical. Of course the most effective way of stopping a horse from crib-biting is to tie his head up in such a way that he cannot get hold of anything to bite. This, however, is obviously not practical because you cannot keep a horse tied up day and night. If, therefore, a crib-biter is worth keeping, the most practical method that I can suggest is to keep him in a stall or loose-box where there is *nothing* on to which he can get his teeth. This is by no means as difficult as it appears. He should be fed from some movable box or other receptacle which should be placed on the floor and moved after the meal.

You will notice that just as with some of the troubles mentioned in the other chapters, what I have written about cribbers, wind-suckers, and weavers are not cures but preventatives. There is no cure for them so far as I know and they are catching. All three vices are very wearing to the horse's system. As bad companions will, cribbing and wind-sucking and sometimes weaving too often go together. And let it be noted that too long confinement in stables, with consequent boredom, is a frequent cause of these vices.

12. *Rolling*

ROLLING under saddle is always a bad thing. It looks dangerous and is certainly uncomfortable for the rider, but actually it rarely does any damage to the rider and certainly none to the horse. There are other disagreeable results, however, and it is something to be stopped altogether if possible.

I remember hunting one day when a friend of mine had a horse that rolled with him. Now horses do this because they are uncomfortable under the saddle. It is not likely that they roll because they have a sore there, though this is possible ; but they get overheated, the hair perhaps is drawn the wrong way, and the saddle becomes uncomfortable. What, therefore, more natural than that they should want to dispossess themselves of the saddle and the rider, and what way more obvious than to rub them both off ? The horse that my friend was riding selected a very large pool of water more like a pond, running out of a cattle yard through which we were passing from one covert to another. The nature of the liquid through which he was passing need not be described, but the horse chose the middle of this to roll in. The rider was not sufficiently experienced to stop this and was too bewildered to get off on to his feet, so he found himself at full length in this unappetizing mixture, with the horse on its back trying to rub the saddle off. This was bad enough, but the trouble was that nobody had the inclination to do much more than sympathize with him (at a distance), certainly not to be over-helpful, and about the best he could do was to pull some straw out of a nearby stack, rub the saddle and himself free from a certain amount of slime, and go home. Because of the smell no one wanted to go anywhere near them.

Fortunately by certain signs and signals a horse will give some indication that he is about to roll, very much as a horse will show its rider when it is about to buck. What he does is a little hard to describe, but if I put it that there is a feeling under you that the horse is about to collapse, this will be sufficient to warn you. When the warning comes, therefore, the only thing to do is—set about the horse, get hold of his head, get hold of him with your heels and with your whip, and do not forget your voice, too. Frighten him out of it. Give it to him rough and drive him on—there is no other way and it is always effective. It may be that you will put the horse off only temporarily from this desire to roll ; but in my experience it is more likely to be permanent for that particular ride or hunt, because for some reason horses do not try again, and one can only assume that the desire to roll is a temporary one.

If your horse should go down—and it may be he is a bit quicker than you are—then, if you are alive enough, you can get off, and it is not likely that you will get your leg or foot even in the slightest degree crushed under the horse. If it should happen that he does get down while you are still mounted, then keep hold of the reins and give him two or three with your stick or whip, preferably about the shoulders and quarters, and your horse will probably forget all about rolling and be only too anxious to get on his legs again. You must, however, do this quickly and with great determination, shouting at him the while.

Apart from rolling in mud there would be nothing very harmful in a horse having a good roll if it were not for the saddle ; but the trouble is that the weight of a horse's body and the violent movement which he exercises during rolling is more than sufficient not only to damage the surface of the saddle but also—what is more serious—to crack the ' tree.' For this reason, if not for any other, rolling should be treated as a serious vice, although it is in fact one of the most natural things to be expected from a horse.

To summarize this chapter on rolling, therefore, let us say that rolling in itself is something about which the rider need have no qualms as to his personal safety, a little thought for his personal convenience, but some considerable concern about the fate of his saddle and, to some extent, his bridle. It is, by the way, a rather humiliating affair, especially if the performance takes place, as it usually does, when hunting, at covert side among a crowd of other horses. A determined bustling with plenty of noise is the way to keep your horse on his feet or to get him on his feet again.

13. *Hard to Box*

IN these days, when there are so many one-horse owners who ' do ' their own horse, how lovely it would be if *all* horses just walked into their boxes to take a journey, whether the box be a railway horse-box, a motor horse-box or a one-horse trailer ! So many of them will, but many of them will not ; and the curious thing is that some horses of exemplary behaviour in all other respects fight shy of horse-boxes. I can understand this, because a horse has sufficient sense to realize that he is not only being asked to go up a ramp and get into a confined space but has also to face the bumps and bangs, the noises and the swaying which must inevitably follow. To expect universal tranquillity and obedience is asking a lot of a simple-minded fellow.

One thing is certain : you cannot drag a horse into a box single-handed or, so far as that goes, with half a dozen helpers. All these people with a difficult horse can gain the desired end by a variety of methods : by blindfolding, by pushing from behind, by pushing sideways, by riding him in (effective but obviously dangerous), and, most effectively of all, by having one person push the horse back on his hocks while two others clasp hands under his quarters and just above his hocks and, by putting their weight to it, literally push him into the box. This, however, requires, as you see, several helpers who are by no means always available, and unless these helpers are horsemen it is hardly likely you will find them prepared to do this.

I have with army horses put dozens into boxes in this way, but one comes across those that really will not allow

'*One thing is certain : you cannot drag a horse into a box.*'

you to do this. This is the type of horse which will fight you, which will kick and rear and twist and turn, and you just cannot get hold of him. How bad, therefore, is the plight of the one-horse owners to whom I have referred, who want to walk their horse quietly into a box to go away for a day's hunting or what you will, and the horse just will not go in. They say to me, ' I cannot box my horse. What can I do ? ' and I find it very difficult to give a helpful answer.

If you want me to produce a remedy for this real ill, I can only suggest the following. It is a good remedy if you have the material to work upon. Let me assume that you have a trailer or can borrow a motor horse-box to experiment with. It may be that you have a yard into which your local motor-transport man can bring in his box and leave it with you from time to time, or you may be able to arrange to visit your horse-box contractor and use a horse-box on his premises. When feeding-time comes round get your sieve or bowl of food, put the halter on your horse and lead him to the box and feed him in the box. If he refuses to go in let him get a bit more hungry and try again later. The more hungry he becomes the more likely it is that he will go into the box for his meal. After he has done this, as he surely will, take him back into his own box or stall, and if possible give him his next meal in the horse-box and his next and his next. You must of course make much of him when you do get him in the box ; and it is a good thing to put some straw over the ramp and when he is feeding in his allotted space to put the ramp up as quietly as you can.

I would like to recall something I once saw which emphasized in my mind that very likely a horse hesitates to go into a horse-box because of a real fear of the unknown.

I was staying in a hotel overlooking the station yard at Minehead during the tournament of the West Somerset Polo Club. A number of ponies were being boxed in the yard, and all successfully but one. This pony put up a big fight, and although there were half a dozen grooms and porters, all looking fairly experienced, the pony beat them and they all went off to breakfast leaving one groom in charge. He stood there with the pony at the foot of the ramp, prepared to wait, I suppose, for the return of the helpers. After a few minutes, as I was finishing my shaving at the window, I saw the pony walk into the box of his own accord, without a sign of encouragement from the remaining groom—indeed almost dragging the man after him. I can only think that the pony looked around, and perhaps smelt around, and came to the conclusion that the box was just as good a spot to stand in as the station yard, so he went in.

14. *Hard to Catch*

WHETHER its cause is playful devilment or whether it is fear, there is no more exasperating habit in a horse than that of evading the man who wants to catch him—and, by the way, few things are more exhausting to the horseman. The dice are heavily loaded in favour of the horse, because few fields are so kindly devised as to contain a trap into which the unfortunate man can hope to drive the more fortunate horse. If such a convenient corner is to be found in the field, then the task is made comparatively easy, but what chance has one individual in an ordinary rectangular field of catching a horse which has just made up his mind for one reason or another not to be caught? It is easy enough to say that you should take a sieve of corn and the battle is more than half won, but countless people have tried this and have failed.

I do believe, however, that this trouble which I am now describing is overcome by the old idea of the master mind exerting itself over the subject horse. It may sound boastful to say that I rarely have any difficulty in catching a horse in a field, but I mention it because I try to approach the horse with a mixture, hard to define, of determination to accomplish what I set out to do, and outward calm and apparent indifference to the job and an appearance of time being no object. Such a mixture is just that which it is necessary to serve up to a horse in these circumstances. One needs a sieve of oats or oats and chaff with a hemp halter so placed (and more or less covered with the chaff) that it can be slipped easily over the horse's head when he drops his nose into the sieve. That sounds very nice and very easy, but I must admit you have got to get near enough to the horse for him to get his nose down ; and for the purpose of being helpful I must assume that you just cannot get near him and none of the wiles or the chasings which you have tried are of any avail whatever.

You have, therefore, what we must admit is an impossible horse to catch, and what are you going to do about it ? As so many people find it necessary to keep horses at grass, either for economy or perhaps because the horses are mountain- or moorland-bred and are better so, a way must be found to make this horse-catching a simple job. You must do one of two things: either hobble your horse or tether him. Of the two I prefer the latter. You must have a long rope attached to his head stall and a really strong iron spike driven heavily into the ground. But I am not suggesting that you should always tether him.

Tether him only for the time being, and when you want to catch him in the morning go out with your sieve of oats or chaff ; and the more attractive it is made by the addition of some sliced carrots or what you will, the better. Let him enjoy two or three minutes with his nose in the sieve and then untether him and lead him away for the ride, tethering him again after.

Repeat this a number of times, and unless I am much mistaken you will find that your horse associates your arrival in the field with something really good to eat. Next time turn him loose in his field when he will probably forget he is untethered and will either let you catch him or, what is more likely, will come to you. Like almost everything connected with horses this requires quite an amount of patience, and it may be much better to keep him tethered this question of how soon he may be a free horse again will depend upon your horse's temperament, and you will be the best judge of that.

Alternatively, and if it is possible, make a pen in one corner of the field and always feed him there. Let him feed there a number of times before your first attempt to catch him.

Do not make the fatal mistake of walking the horse out of the field directly you have put the bridle on, when, perhaps, he has had only a mouthful out of the sieve. Play the game and give him a chance of eating up the lot. You will then find it much easier to catch him the next time.

'Likely to receive a dangerous fall.'

15. *Stumbling*

AT first thought few people would agree that stumbling in a horse is a vice, and this is true enough. It arises from a number of causes. Bad conformation much more often than not means bad action, which is a definite cause of stumbling, and because of this it is obvious that no permanent cure can be effected. Bad shoeing, too, will cause a horse to stumble, and, of course, anything in the nature of disease of the feet and weakness there will lead to the trouble, and it is a very dangerous one too. Weakness of condition and going on the forehand are common causes of stumbling. It is admitted by all horsemen that a rider is much more likely to receive a dangerous fall through a stumbling horse than when thrown from the saddle at speed.

Weak horses and those of generally poor constitution are obviously liable to come down, especially on uneven ground. They will roll about and drag their feet, and the rider on such a horse will be lucky if he does not come to grief sooner or later—probably much sooner. There are horses, too, which will look about them, and the result is very much as with the man or woman who strides along without looking where he or she is going.

Whatever the cause, bad conformation, weakness, or going about with head in air, great improvement can be made by the rider. A horse, then, that shows this tendency to stumble must always be ridden much more collectedly than your good mover. He must be ridden more up into his bridle and his hocks must be kept better under him.

It will usually be found that the type of horse that we are dealing with is sluggish, and it would be better to ride him with blunt spurs. He should receive plenty of assistance from your heels. While I am on the subject of heels I would like to point this out : do not get into the habit, as many riders do, of continually 'heeling' your horse. There are many, and goodish riders too, who will ride a horse continuously with heel taps or at least inter-mittent calf pressure. At every stride the heel taps the flanks and one can only suppose that in doing so the rider thinks he is collecting the horse and keeping him collected. Actually this is not so, because after a while a horse becomes completely insensitive to the feel of the heel. It should be applied only from time to time when the rider feels that the horse is going out of collection.

To continue the cure : there is nothing better for sharpening up a horse and making him take care of his feet, which is after all what is required in the case of these stumblers, than to trot him smartly over rough ground. Take him off the beaten track wherever it is possible, turn him on to a rough field or through a bit of plough and make him step sharply. It can be assumed that horses do not like to stumble, and therefore if your lesson is such that it makes the horse look after itself it is all to the good.

There is nothing better, too, than to ride a horse down a steep slope, the steeper (within reason) the better, and in soft going let it be at a sharp trot. Actually you need not have any particular qualms about this because any horse will take wonderful care of himself in such circumstances, and the horse of bad conformation is no exception.

Incidentally, I have several times heard people, who presume to know something about horses, advocate that under no circumstances should a horse go down any hill faster than at a walk. This, to my mind, takes first place in stupid remarks. Hunters are certainly not ridden across level ground, and what about our mountain and moorland breeds ?

A bad stumbler may well be a hopeless case, and it would probably be better to dispose of him ; but I am convinced that a great amount of improvement can be effected if such a horse is ridden with determination on the lines I have suggested. He must, however, be reasonably well fed and free from any diseases of the feet. To expect an underfed horse, or one suffering from chronic or even temporary lameness, to go well and cleanly and soundly is to expect the impossible.

And just another few words. Many horses infested with red worms will stumble and drag the toe. The remedy for this is obvious and startling in its effectiveness.

16. *Jump-shy*

To be shy of jumping is certainly not a vice, but then the same remark can be applied to being water-shy. It is, however, not really a question of training but of introducing confidence in a horse, for there must be something in the mentality of a jump-shy horse that causes him to stick his toes in the ground when asked to jump. This is the more certain because in my experience the great majority of horses really do enjoy jumping in the hunting-field.

Over and over again people have written to me that otherwise well-trained horses just will not jump, and how are they to overcome this difficulty ? With this trouble I couple the related one of horses that will not go through gaps in hedges, a most exasperating habit.

It is not difficult to teach a horse to jump because, as I

say, he has a natural liking for it. The trouble most inexperienced people have is that it is very difficult to make a horse jump unless the rider has complete confidence in his own ability to do so. If you have this then you will convey it to your horse. No doubt the best way to make an unwilling horse jump or go through a gap is in the first instance to lead him over very small jumps or even poles or other similar obstacles *on the ground*, increasing the size of the obstacle from time to time.

If an older horse starts to refuse his jumps where he had previously caused no difficulty, do the same thing to him, which amounts to re-schooling. Lead him over the obstacles and lunge him over very small jumps. When riding over them take the greatest possible care to see that you do not interfere with his mouth. This jump-shyness in a mature horse is, you may be sure, the result of unsympathetic treatment over jumps in the past ; and you must make him forget such treatment.

A gap-shy horse probably needs the confidence of its rider. Although you cannot pull a horse through a gap, he will most likely follow you if you walk through yourself first, holding him on a long rein. If he will not do this, spend a few minutes in the gap as unconcernedly as possible. He will go through in the end ; he only needs to see that there is nothing to fear. If time presses and you must get on, turn him round, mounted or unmounted, and back him through.

Unfortunately it is the easiest thing in the world to put a horse off jumping, and if you have succeeded in making your horse jump you must do all you possibly can to foster the enjoyment he gets out of it. You can do this by a negative approach. There is one thing that most horses suffer at the hands of their riders. and that is a jab in the

A jump-shy horse.

mouth. It takes a very insensitive horse to stand up to this and still go on jumping surely and confidently, and no one should be afraid of holding by one hand to the breast piece or some form of neck strap, thus leaving the horse with a free rein. Even the most highly trained jumpers cannot be relied upon to take off so evenly that the rider can be assured of going with his horse, nor can the best rider guarantee that he will not be ' left behind ' (in other words, behind the line of balance) at a jump. How much less, therefore, can one rely upon an unschooled horse and a not very experienced rider ! Consequently the neck strap I have mentioned is really invaluable.

This chapter has resolved itself into instructions on schooling horses over jumps. I had some hesitation in including jump-shyness among the horse vices, but no hack is really a good hack unless it can go over reasonable obstacles and through any fair opening that may be asked of it. To allow a horse to develop this disinclination is to encourage something which may grow to be a vice, and so I think this chapter has a place here.

17. *Bed-eating*

THIS may be a case for the vet, and vice may not come into it at all. But, on the other hand, vet or no vet, it may develop into a vice ; and like so many habits that are likely to become evil it should be tackled and cured, as it can be.

But, first of all : people make a lot of fuss about horses eating a bit of their straw bedding, which, of course, is or should be wheat-straw bedding. There is nothing really harmful about straw as something for a horse to eat, certainly in strict moderation, so long as he is not expected to do fast work ; and picking up a bit of straw here and there from the bed is not likely to affect him. The trouble of course is that if a horse starts to eat his bedding he will as likely as not eat it in increasing quantities, which is a bad thing and a habit that may grow from bad to worse. By this I mean that a horse is almost sure to pick up bedding that he has soiled and then most obviously it is not good for him. Worse than this, the habit may develop into a depraved taste for soiled bedding. Many horses have acquired this disgusting habit, and we must do all we can to stop it.

If I had a horse that really did develop the bed-eating habit I should first of all test him for worms. Worms, as you probably know, are the cause of an unnatural appetite, and therefore you should find out whether he has them. You may have a man who is able to dose the horse properly for worms, and it is much better that he should have a full and reliable dose and that a good job should be made of it. You may even be able to do it yourself, but I recommend that you should go to your vet for the purpose. If worms are found then we will hope that after the dose the bad habit will cease to exist.

If after this has been tried the horse still eats his bed, consider whether he is sufficiently fed. A great many horses do not get enough to eat, or more particularly do not get it at the time when they need it. Being hungry, what more natural than that they should put their heads down and pick up some straw, especially as hay that has fallen from the rack or the net is so often mingled with the straw ? Try to find out *when* the horse eats his bed and see whether he has cleaned up his meal. If he has, then add to the ration of that meal each day and watch the effect.

Remember too, in this connection, that a horse is a very big eater at night, and it may be that in the early hours of the morning, when you are not with him, he is having a good meal of bedding. Therefore if your horse is a known bed-eater see that he has a completely ample ration of hay.

Another thing you should consider is whether your horse has become tired of his ordinary daily rations of food on account of its monotony. If a horse literally gets fed up with the same old round of meals without any variation it will soon induce in him a strong desire for something different, so down will go his head again to the unclean stuff which lies about his feet. That brings me to another point. It is natural for a horse to eat off the ground. So you will be helping to cure your horse of this vice if you feed him, at any rate during the course of the cure, off the ground. A good, stout, heavy, wooden box makes quite a good manger and as it is movable it can easily be cleaned.

Now all these things are helpful suggestions to bring your horse back to being a normal feeder, but if it is a bad case, at any rate for a time, I suggest the following. Give your horse a good, full meal, and when he has cleaned it up or appears to have really satisfied his appetite put a muzzle on him. This can be procured from any saddler and is not expensive. Before you do this it would be as well that you should make the bedding unpalatable. This can be done in a number of ways, but I suggest that a good way is to mix some strong—non-poisonous, of course—disinfectant into a weak solution with water, sprinkle it generously over the straw and watch the effect. If the horse's appetite is not too depraved a substitute for straw bedding can be used in the form of peat-moss litter or sawdust. They both have advantages and also unfortunately considerable disadvantages as well. Peat-moss cakes very badly and makes mucking-out a real labour. Sawdust cakes to some extent and cannot be used where the stables are drained, as the drains will surely become blocked.

As a final word, do not worry about a horse that just picks at a bit of straw now and again—it will not hurt him ; just watch and see that the picking does not become whole-sale consumption.

18. *Toe-dragging*

HERE is a trouble that afflicts young horses and some of the older ones too. It is surprising how many people write to me and talk about their nicely bred horses who are so good in every way—except that they *will* drag their hind legs, wearing out the toes of their shoes and causing an unnecessary number of visits to the forge.

Bad conformation may have something to do with this ; weak hocks, badly let down hocks, and particularly sickle hocks. It may be bad conformation in other parts also, because a horse that goes uncollected will be leaving his quarters behind him ; and it follows that all movement, coming as it then will in the main from the forehand, is placing upon it the burden of carrying the quarters to a large extent with it. If you are satisfied that your horse goes uncollected, then see if you cannot balance him up by the use of aids behind the girths, in other words by pressure of the calves and the use of the heels. This, of course, should be made to synchronize with the aids applied to the forehand through the reins. This chapter is not a lesson on schooling, which would take many chapters ; but you should certainly satisfy yourself whether or not your horse goes unbalanced if you are to cure this toe-dragging.

More likely than not your horse does this through weakness. Does he get enough to eat? Does he get the right kind of stuff to eat? And if he does, then does he digest his food properly? Look to his droppings. They should, as you know, be of such consistency that they just have a tendency to crumble or break when they fall to the ground. If they seem to be wrong then see your vet. The horse's teeth may need attention, he may have worms—but your vet will satisfy himself on these two points and in any other way that his skilled knowledge suggests.

The trouble at any rate arises from one of these two causes or both—bad conformation, or food that is insufficient or wrong. Whichever the cause may be (and if it is insufficient food, then the extra feeding will bring him up to the proper physical standard) you can help matters greatly by giving him the kind of exercise that will strengthen those muscles which may be at the root cause of the trouble. Not only, as I have said before, should the horse be ridden into a balanced horse—and every horse should be ridden in this way—but also make a point of riding him uphill and downhill on every possible occasion. I do not mean by this, of course, that you should sicken him by climbing up and climbing down, but let him do plenty of hill work, and in going downhill ' shake him out ' and let him slip down at a decent pace. You can do this with assurance, because not only will he be getting his hocks under him and be bringing his muscles into play, but he will also take very good care of himself and of you in the process. It may be you live in flat country and nothing like a hill worthy of the name is to be found for miles ; a good substitute then is to ride him over a cavaletti. This is rather like a series of very large wooden carving knife and fork rests, laid one in front of the other, six to a dozen perhaps

They can be of equal distance one from the other or of varying distances, but I prefer them to be of equal distance and about six feet apart. Ride your horse two or three times up and down this before you take him out to exercise and the same on his return. This will have a wonderful effect in strengthening his hocks and bringing his toes well off the ground.

19. *Overbending*

THIS 'overbentness' in a horse is not a vice, but it is an awkward 'accomplishment' which should be rectified if possible. I think 'accomplishment' is not a bad word to use because the horse which is overbent to an extreme has certainly achieved quite an impressive position for his head, and one which might be thought difficult to acquire. With a discussion upon the overbent horse it is quite fitting that we should consider the opposite type, which is the horse that takes all its weight on its head and forehand, and might not improperly be described as the underbent horse. At any rate, a consideration of the overbent horse and how to cure him is made more easy by a criticism of his opposite number.

The horse becomes overbent either from bad 'making' in his early stages or through bad conformation. An overbent horse is a horse that, in simple words, carries his chin on his chest. Among the inexperienced are those who, far from disliking such a head carriage, think that it gives the horse a courageous and gay appearance ; and to some extent I agree with them.

The trouble, however, with these overbent horses is that they rather have you in their power, because it is surprising

'He is moving all the time too much on his hocks.'

what a lot of fun a horse can have (from his point of view) when he is really overbent. Having his chin tucked well into his chest he is in a position to take charge and may very well sail away with you to your extreme discomfort, not to say danger.

The reverse of the overbent horse is the one which pokes his nose right into his bridle and goes heavily on the forehand, invariably giving a dead weight on the hands. Of the two I prefer the overbent horse, especially as fortunately he is very rarely as dangerous as I have perhaps led you to understand, and he does not, in the ordinary way, present any great problem to the experienced rider. The difference between these two types is that the overbent horse is moving all the time too much on his hocks, whereas the horse that leans into his bridle is probably always going heavily on his forehand—making for a most uncomfortable ride in every way, for not only is his going rough and jarring, but also, as his nose is poked out and his mouth usually insensitive, control of any sort is reduced to a minimum.

The cure for the overbent horse really amounts almost to remaking. First the horse must be encouraged to reach out his head and to lengthen his neck. He must be ridden with the least possible pressure upon the mouth, giving him freedom from his bridle and so releasing the muscles of the neck and helping him to carry not only the neck but the head as well in the correct position. At the same time he must be made to go more on the forehand and less on the hocks. To encourage the correct head and neck carriage, and also to synchronize better the movement of the forehand with that of the quarters, the horse must be driven up into his bridle by pressure of the rider's lower leg behind the girth, or of the rider's heels, which must be kept low and close into the horse's side behind the girths. I prefer at the same time—

to correct the balance which in these overbent horses is obviously at fault—to lean perceptibly forward, thereby compelling the horse to take more weight upon his forehand of which he has up to then been apparently shy. This ' unloosening ' of the horse and the correcting of its balance is a matter which must take up much time and requires much patience, but wonderful improvement can be made even with a horse of bad conformation.

As contrasted with the cure for the overbent horse, the heavily fronted horse, or whatever may be the best term to use, must have his hocks brought up to you and his forehand brought back to you. In other words, heels and hands must work in unison. More sense will be obtained with this latter type of horse if he is worked in a confined space and twisted and turned about as much as possible, halted and sent on again, swung round on his hocks, and made to jump into a canter from a standstill, which obviously lightens his forehand. The overbent horse, however, is much better worked in a straight line during his remaking lessons.

There is this to be said about these two disagreeable forms of gait. They are both wearing to the horse, but each in a different way. There is no doubt that this unnatural overbending of the neck—as distinct from bending from the poll, which forms the correct head carriage—places a considerable strain upon the horse's neck muscles ; and, although I may be wrong, I think that in the overbent horse we find a good deal of wear going on to its temperament, for he is usually gassy and up on his toes. With the other type the weight is thrown upon the forelegs ; which, with the low, long, and heavy neck carriage, puts an undue proportion of weight on to the forelegs. The front of a horse being considerably heavier than the back portion, it will be seen that a horse going abnormally heavy on his forehand accentuates this disparity.

20. *Unwise to Bridling*

AT first glance this may appear to be not only a clumsy title but also not very illuminating. I am of course proposing to deal with the horse that has not been made bridle-wise—or, as many describe it, used to neck-reining. Whichever title you prefer, the bridle-wise horse is that which answers to the indirect rein rather than the direct rein. This requires some explanation.

You are mounted and proceeding on your way, and you wish to turn into a gate on your left-hand side. If you are riding a horse that is not bridle-wise you naturally exert some feel or pressure on the left rein, and the horse turns into the gate—good, he has done what was expected of him. Now if you are riding a bridle-wise horse, then instead of pulling the left-hand rein (which is here called the direct rein) you do not move your hand on the reins but pass your hand to the left so that the *right* rein lies with a certain amount of pressure over the right-hand side of the horse's neck, thus giving with it obviously a certain amount of pull on that rein (here called the indirect rein). A horse that is properly bridle-wise will immediately lay his head and neck somewhat to the left—in other words, will bend towards or tend to face the gate which you are aiming for, and pass in.

The inexperienced horseman may from this consider that it is quite immaterial which method is used, and so far as the ultimate result is concerned it *is* quite immaterial ; but there are the greatest advantages in making a horse bridle-wise ; indeed so much so that I would never ride

81

a horse of my own which was not schooled to neck-rein.

Just consider a few of the advantages. The bridle-wise horse is infinitely more versatile—he can be twisted and turned about with one hand with the greatest ease ; but with a horse not so trained it is obvious that both the rider's hands have to be available, so that either may be used according to which side the horse has to be guided. In the ordinary way of hacking this is not a particular hardship, but although probably most people have both hands on the reins most of the time, there are very many occasions when only one hand is available, as for instance when a gate has to be opened, the branch of a tree pushed aside, or the horse edged away from an obstruction, at the same time as one wishes to turn. Remember too, that one often has to handle one's hunting whip for various purposes into which I need not go, and in playing polo of course one hand only is available for the reins, making it absolutely necessary to ride a bridle-wise pony.

Above nearly all other reasons I think that the sheer *comfort* of riding such a horse is the biggest recommendation for it. The novice who has ridden only a horse accustomed to the direct pull can have no idea of the difference and pleasure obtained from riding a bridle-wise horse.

The owner of the incompletely trained horse, for that is really what the animal understanding only the direct pull is, may take heart ; for there is nothing easier than to teach a horse to be bridle-wise, and this he will learn very quickly. To turn him to the left, take your reins in your left hand and hold them at moderate length, that is to say not too short and not too long, and place them, as I have mentioned before, to the left, so that some little pressure lies to the right-hand side of his neck. At the same time exert some pressure with the left heel behind the girth. You will

' *In playing polo it is absolutely necessary to ride a bridle-wise pony.*'

realize that you are pulling his head to the left and urging his quarters to the right. At first he may be unyielding but he will come to it after a time. As soon as he moves well over to the left hand, reverse the movement to get him going in the opposite direction by placing the reins over to the right-hand side and exerting the pressure with the right heel. In other words, left hand left heel, right hand right heel. You should aim not only to turn him to the left or to the right but should allow the pressure of hand and heel to remain until he has turned a circle on either hand.

Here is a tip which will make the lesson still more easy. Let somebody stand at your horse's head when you first try the above, and when you turn him to the left get your assistant to place his hand on the right-hand side of your horse's head as you place your left hand to the left. Obviously by doing so he is just pushing the horse's head round to the left, in other words in the direction required. He should of course work from the opposite side when you are turning the horse to the right. I mention this method because it obviously assists the horse to let him know just what is required by this indirect rein pressure, for he may not take to it right away.

In conclusion I cannot impress upon you too much what an advantage you will gain by riding a bridle-wise horse. Let me point out that there have been countless occasions when horsemen who have been riding or more frequently hunting on bridle-wise horses have been saved from many nasty accidents, perhaps even worse, by being able to twist and turn infinitely quicker than by the direct-rein method. Believe me, it is a safety method if ever there was one ; it makes the horse one hundred per cent mobile.

21. *Tongue Over Bit*

BEING at sea in a ship which has parted with her rudder must be rather like riding a horse with his tongue over the bit ; at least, I imagine, that must represent the very essence of helplessness. Although a horse which has placed its tongue over the bit is not quite as bad as that, there is no doubt the rider suffers from a very uneasy feeling of partial helplessness.

To begin with, such a horse is not responsive to neck-reining ; he certainly will not place his head and neck in the true position, but instead probably pokes his nose and refuses to close his mouth, and, in particular, is much inclined to pull. Indeed a horse that carries the bit under the tongue instead of over it is half-way to being a puller.

This trouble is brought about by some form of injury within the mouth. Either the horse has received some damage to the tongue, which has become sore, possibly pinched or even cut, or it has damaged the bars of its mouth, which have become calloused, and he prefers to carry the bit there rather than upon the tongue. Whichever it may be, something must be done if possible to relieve the pain and to induce the horse to carry the bit in the normal position which, as we all know, is upon the tongue.

Perhaps the first thing to do is to ride the horse in the easiest bit possible, the bar of which should be covered with rubber and have some pattern of port-shaped mouth, to give more room for the tongue. It is obvious that with such an uncomfortable arrangement as a bit in a horse's mouth, nothing can contribute more to easing the discomfort than something which is soft to the touch. Care must be taken to see that the bit is large enough for the mouth. (So many horses are, unhappily, ridden with bits that are too narrow, and so a pinching of the lips takes place which causes distress to a horse and makes him worry and fuss to find some means of meeting the trouble ; and possibly putting his tongue over the bit is his answer.) If this is ineffective, you can use the gridiron bit, pressure upon which causes the grid to rise, forming an obstacle over which he finds it difficult to place his tongue, and which, if he does, causes him discomfort or pain. A bit with a high port has much the same effect ; and a Kineton noseband is also much used and is a good attachment to a bit because it is also effective in stopping a horse from boring and pulling.

A simple and very effective arrangement, which is used quite a lot, is to tie a piece of cord or a bootlace to the centre of the bar of the bit, passing the ends (which should be of equal length) out on each side of the mouth, and attaching both ends to the centre of the noseband.

Where possible I recommend that, if you have a horse that puts its tongue over the bit, you should try to find out where the trouble is in the mouth ; whether it is on the tongue or the bars. If this is very clearly shown then, if possible, the horse should not be ridden, so that every opportunity is given for the trouble to clear up ; assist this if you can by some healing treatment. I do not recommend tying down the tongue, which method is sometimes used, for this must give much quite unnecessary distress and goes nowhere towards curing the trouble. No horse that I know of is incurable ; and while the trouble lasts, the horse is a potential danger.

I need hardly say that the horse should be ridden with the lightest possible hands and that it should be ridden with every consideration. Have in mind, therefore, whether your horse is of an excitable, headstrong character ; and if he is, confine your outings, when you know there is a certain soreness in the mouth, to walking or slow trotting. Cantering, as we know, is to the excitable horse an encouragement to further efforts. The effect of such excitement is cumulative and may lead to a horse being really 'hotted up', throwing his head about, fighting the bit and adding to the damage.

22. *Unwilling to Stand*

How few English horses are to be found that will allow the rider to dismount and then remain standing even when the rider has walked away. We are all familiar with the cowboys' horses in the Western films which gallop into the picture and are reined up on their hocks while the cowboy dismounts and rushes up the steps into the saloon with a pistol in each hand. Sometimes he will loosely throw the ends of the reins a couple of times around the hitching rail, but often enough the horse is just dismounted and remains standing. There is no fake about this, nor is it difficult to effect ; the horses are trained to remain entirely stationary, and it is a question only of training.

All those of us who follow hounds are familiar with the sight at a kill, or when a fox has gone to ground, of the huntsman and whipper-in dismounting and pulling the reins over the horse's head and throwing the loop over a post or the twigs of a bush. The result is quite effective ; the horse will remain put and does not attempt to get clear and move away, though it is certain that in the majority of cases, especially where some branch is used, the merest pull would set him free. The psychological effect on the horse's mind

'The horse will remain put.'

is that he is tethered and that is the end of it ; and he must remain where he stands. How convenient this is ! For, ninety-nine times out of a hundred, the ordinary rider when he dismounts and needs to move from one place to another always has to lead his horse about with him. The two apparently must be inseparable, however awkward it may be.

The way to teach a horse to stand is to put him in a strong, closely fitting head-collar with a longish tough rope attached, and to tether him to something really fixed and solid *on the ground.* This may be the upright post of a fence, a really heavy and more or less immovable log, or anything else he cannot shift, such as a plough or a harrow. Then walk away from the horse and see what the effect is. It is to be hoped that he will fight against this restraint and discover that he cannot get free. If this is so, you have made a definite start in the schooling ; and you should lead him away and tie him up to something else equally solid. Repeat this often and make sure that he is fastened to something that is going to hold him well and truly. Put his bridle on then—perhaps another day—but with a head-collar underneath, and repeat the same schooling. When he ceases, as he will after a while, to put up any form of resistance, you have probably succeeded in what you set out to do. For safety's sake and to avoid any possible trouble you might, when you are feeling fairly sure of your horse, leave off the head-collar but attach to one side of the bit a fairly strong cord rather than the reins themselves, for if something does go wrong it would be a pity that they should be broken. Finally, on the last ' tying-up ', throw the reins over the horse's head, for the ideal is that a horse should stand untethered and with the ends of the reins on the ground. There is a definite reason for pulling them over his head rather than leaving them lying upon the neck or over the saddle, because unquestionably the horse associates reins or a halter lying from his head to the ground with the control which he knows it is useless to fight against.

You may think it is hardly worthwhile to go to this bother, for no one can suggest that it is a vice for a horse not to stand ; on the other hand think how very convenient it is to have a horse that you can confidently leave standing and on how many occasions this will be helpful to you and a cause of satisfaction. If you have the spirit of real horse-manship and the wish to bring your horse as near as possible to perfection, then try out all I have written in this chapter—and succeed. You will, when you have emulated the Westerner, at least have the satisfaction of having trained your horse to do something which I am sorry to say not one English horse in thousands will do. Like so many other things where man and horse are concerned, this calls for man's patient endeavour in simple things.

23. *Rug-stripping*

PERHAPS this vice ought to have been included in my chapter ' Bad Stable Manners ' ; perhaps it is hardly worthy of one all to itself, for it is not very prevalent. Yet I am certain if you looked over the rugs, particularly the night rugs, in any riding-school stable you would find many that were torn, especially round about the collar, and that the tears certainly did not come about by the carelessness of the grooms. Some horses will in a very short time tear their rugs to pieces, and they usually do this at night. Others will not exactly damage the rug ; but when visiting them in the morning you will find them draped in their rugs in the

most fantastic fashion, the whole thing twisted round, sometimes pulled up on the neck and sometimes even round the
head—and many a horse has been found in the morning
with the rug pulled right over its head, and lying on the
floor with the surcingle left behind !

There is not necessarily a reason for this, though it may
well be that the horse has a sensitive skin, and that when it
is ' hotted up ' under the rug, irritation is caused. ' Hotting-
up ' is especially likely if, when the horse lies down, he gets
the rug in an uncomfortable position ; and nobody can say
that a horse lies gracefully, nor that he lowers himself to the
ground in a way calculated to keep his rug smoothly and
comfortably under his surcingle.   In other words he is rather
an uncouth fellow when he lies down in bed.   What is much
more likely, however, is that rug-stripping or -biting—
especially the latter—is just a bad habit brought on by
something which is hard to discover and which is a matter
only for conjecture.   Boredom probably has much to do with
it ; or perhaps digestive trouble or some other sort of inconvenience ; and it is hard to say whether any cure can be found.

We must look, then, for a means anyway of keeping the
rug on the horse's back and preventing it from being torn to
pieces.   The thing that suggests itself at once, of course, is a
muzzle.   This is no doubt usually effective, but a muzzle is
not a very nice thing to leave on a horse's head all night,
and unless it is properly adjusted he may rub it half off and
perhaps get into some sort of trouble or mischief with it.   A
more effective way is to have firmly stitched on to the head-
collar, well on the rear behind the noseband, a piece of stout
leather about a quarter of an inch thick, about four inches deep
and about three inches broad ; in other words of such a size
that it falls down well below the line of the teeth. The actual
measurements of course depend upon how low or how high

the noseband is fitted to the head-stall. The fitment is in a sense rather like a baby's bib, and the idea is that when a horse swings his head back in order to take a snatch at his rug all he can snatch at is the surface of the ' bib ', which of course he can't lay hold of, or even if he can he is not going to do any damage. Properly adjusted this device is fool-proof. I have never experimented with it, but I think it is natural to suppose that in the course of time a horse would give up snatching at his rug when he found he could not lay hold of it, and then the ' bib ' can be discarded.

There is one other way of stopping this trouble, but I do not really recommend it because it is hardly kind to the horse. What I have in mind is a neck cradle. You have perhaps seen this worn by a horse which has some injury, or more likely has been treated with some dressing of an irritating character so that it is necessary to keep him from biting or rubbing the affected part. The cradle consists of a series of rounded pieces of wood strung together at intervals and put round his neck, the ends of the wood pointing respectively to the top of the head and the shoulder. It would hardly seem fair to keep a horse in this all night, as he might quite properly wish to swing his head round and rub himself many times during the night.

24. *Hard to Canter*

SOME while ago a young pony club member wrote to me that at a rally she had been in great trouble because she had much difficulty in making her pony canter. The woman who was examining the class had apparently been very annoyed with the child because she had used her heels vigorously on the pony when she should, according to the examiner, have squeezed the pony behind the girths. That, it seems, would have had the desired effect and the pony would at once have broken into a canter. The child was most indignant, for, she said, ' I can squeeze my pony just as hard as I possibly can and it will make not the slightest difference.' This young member's trouble is the trouble of so many people who ride horses and ponies which are not well schooled. They get into the habit of trotting, and it is really difficult to make them break into a canter.

I am very sympathetic with this young person, especially as I got into the same trouble myself. In my book *Riding for All*, where I was specially dealing with this type of pony, I insisted that heels must be used ; and someone who reviewed the book took me to task and, like the lady examiner, said that I should have advocated squeezing with the calves of my legs. That is useless, and it is a ridiculous form of instruction. Of course, with a well-schooled pony you squeeze it behind the girths and it answers at once ; but with a certain type you could squeeze until you broke the pony's ribs (if you could) and it would not have any effect.

It is with the horse which will not break from a trot that I am dealing in this chapter, and a bad case of this is somewhat difficult to cure. Whether he goes in that fashion owing to bad conformation or whether he does it for preference or for both reasons it is hard to say. But he gets too much on his forehand and leaves his hocks behind, and you must do what you can to bring the two together, indeed to bring the hocks so far under him that in order to balance himself he has to canter—and you must of course help him with this. Probably if you were riding with spurs and carried a whip, a touch with the spur on the near side behind the girth and a touch with the whip down the quarters on the same side would make him break readily into a canter.

'The horse which will not break from a trot.'

Many, however, prefer not to ride with spurs and do not care to hit a horse, though the application of a blunt spur and the laying-on of a stick not too hard certainly does no harm to any horse. In the absence of these I recommend that while the horse is trotting he should be driven up into his bridle with the heels, while at the same time his forehand is reined back in order to bring together the two ends, as it were ; and that at the psychological moment, which must be chosen by the rider, he should receive a strong application of the heel on the near side, the rider at the same time raising and turning the head slightly with the left rein.

This may or may not be sufficient ; I hope it will be. There is something else which can be done to assist. I feel that the whole process of breaking a horse into a canter is helped by some vigorous riding from the seat of the rider. Until the hoped-for moment of cantering arrives, the rider should sit down in the saddle and help to induce the canter by a slight but firm circular movement of the body anti-clockwise. I do not mean that the rider should be swinging himself round in the saddle—and from the onlooker's point of view the movement should be almost imperceptible—but if you will think out carefully what I have said you will, I think, understand what I mean.

I have ridden a great number of horses of what may be called the riding-school type—horses which have been spoilt in their gait and their manners and go very much on their own lines—and I know that this trouble of which I write is a real one. Many people who are not accustomed to this type and ride only well-schooled horses may look with a disdainful eye upon this line of instruction, but I know how exasperating the hard-trotting horse is and how difficult the fault is to correct.

25. *Kicking*

THIS is the chapter I did not want to write, a chapter I had at one time decided not to write, for the very good reason that I know of no real cure for the kicker. I am referring not to the horse that kicks at you in his stable, or indeed at any other time, but the one that kicks at other horses—a dreadful and most dangerous fellow. The number of horses' legs broken and damaged and of bodies cut and torn in the course of a year is very large, and we all know the grievous accidents which happen to so many people in the hunting-field through horses lashing out. It is all very well to say that it is the fault of the person damaged because he should not ride on top of another horse, but we all know that at times in the hunting-field it is almost impossible to keep a horse's length away from another rider.

There are confirmed kickers, really dangerous horses, which of course should never be out in company with others, but then again there are those horses which are only occasional kickers and perhaps will be known to kick only once or twice. I hunted a mare for many seasons which was of impeccable behaviour—I never knew her to kick any horse or show any dislike to other horses with which she might happen to be. But once at the end of a long hunt in company with a stable companion—and both must certainly have been on the tired side—for no reason at all she let drive at the other horse. Fortunately it was a spent kick and no damage was done. Why did she do it? She had not the vice of kicking, and it is hard to say what caused her to do it, unless it was that in some way and for some unknown cause she was fed up with her companion, just as the tempers of human beings become frayed and flare up. In this chapter, however, I am not concerned with these very occasional kickers but with those which have in full measure this really horrible vice.

Having my own ideas about a possible cure but being very uncertain in my own mind, I have discussed the matter with quite a number of knowledgeable people, and not one could tell me what he considered to be a cure. One friend who has spent a lifetime with horses said the only cure that he knew was to turn the culprit out—without shoes of course —with a couple of other well-known kickers, which must also of course be shoeless ! What would be the result of these three vicious animals blazing away at each other I do not know. A considerable amount of damage would be done even without shoes, and I should imagine the one that kicked the hardest, though he *might* break the other two of kicking, would return a greater kicker than ever ! Anyway I doubt whether the others would be cured, and I think it is much more likely that when in company with another horse they would think, ' Here's a horse that may start kicking ; let's get one in first.' It is a possible cure but one which I do not propose to try nor to recommend.

Another very well-known man in the horse world told me that the only effective way to tackle the job was to back the kicker into the first thing you could find, preferably something solid like a brick wall, a tree, a gate, a thorn bush or thick, strong hedge. Run him backward as hard as you can and jam him into it and do it several times. In theory I think this is sound, but in practice the odds are that this convenient obstacle is not likely to be found. Yet I think the chances of a measure of success are good enough to try this method, as I do not think it can do any harm and is not likely to cause any damage to horse or rider.

The majority of knowledgeable people seem to think that the only effective way is to give to the kicker, the moment he lets drive, a real proper lacing, to hit him hard several times, giving him the punishment that he should and probably would associate with the kick which he gave. This method savours of the horseman of the old school, whose methods, from the early days of breaking the youngster, were much more forceful than those practised by the modern school of horsemanship. Some of those with whom I have talked, however, thought that a method of that sort was of not the slightest use and only tended to make a bad-tempered horse —and after all a good-tempered horse does not kick—the more vicious. They unfortunately could not produce an alternative cure, and so their opinion for the purposes for which I have written this book, which is to help all who own a problem horse, can be of no great value to us. I am quite at a loss to give any definite advice and I can only ask you to make what you can of what I have written and to form your own opinion. If I must decide, my inclination is to punish the kicker. I have done it often and I should not like to say that it has necessarily effected a cure, but then I have never ridden a confirmed kicker repeatedly and I would never own one. To ride such an animal is simply to ask for trouble, and it is not fair to those who hunt or hack with us, or to their horses. I believe in principle that immediate punishment must in the horse's mind be associated with the crime, in fact with the kick which he has just delivered. Many disagree with corporal punishment for children, arguing that everything can be done by reasoning ; but you cannot reason with a horse, and if you will ride a kicker, and no one can give you a cure, then I say punish him on the instant and bang him back into anything you can find, and good luck to you if you effect a cure.

'A dreadful and most dangerous fellow.'

In the foregoing chapters I have produced a possible cure for each of the other troubles with which horses are beset, but I conclude this chapter having to admit that I know of no means of stopping the kicker, which has unquestionably the worst of all vices. It is ten to one that any skilful rider can clear himself from the back of a rearer if he is going over. The horse that rolls always gives you plenty of time to get away. The jibber is mostly nothing more than a confounded nuisance, and the runaway, unless he is a real madman, can usually be pulled up or will stick his toes into the ground when he comes to an obstacle—and any decent horseman can be ready for the moment when the horse claps on the brakes. And so on and so forth with your Problem Horse. But so far as I am concerned the kicker has the last word. He is, in fact, the problem to which there is no solution.

26. *Biting and Savaging*

FORTUNATELY savaging is so rarely come across that it is
almost unnecessary to mention it. That you will ever meet
a savage horse is extremely unlikely and so far as I know this
really horrible business is confined to stallions. What
happens is that a horse is seized with what is apparently
an attack of madness, which is recurrent, and simply goes
for the nearest human being with teeth and forelegs—just
tears at the flesh, clothing, anything it can lay its teeth into.
I have never seen a horse savage a man, but a few years ago
I appeared in court to give evidence on the measure of
control required for stallions in hand, the stallion disposi-
tion and so on. In this case, the attack was on a racing lad
in a trainer's establishment and a very nasty business it was
too. This vice or madness is incurable and it is thought the
tendency to it is hereditary.

Biting and 'snatching' however, are two very different
things and are largely induced by thoughtless treatment. A
generation is now growing up which hardly knew the
tradesman's horse and cart, the dairyman's and baker's
delivery ponies. Those who did know them, say between
the wars, and of course before then, will remember that
many wore muzzles indicating the biters. This habit was
acquired through well-meaning people feeding them at the
curb-side. As a result, the ponies hopefully stuck out their
noses to any passer-by, many of whom, out of annoyance,
or fearing an attempt at biting, gave them a smack on the
nose, which of course developed the bad tempered biting
pony.

Snatching and biting are all too prevalent and I should
say that most people accept them as inevitable. The

snatching, which can result in torn clothes or perhaps a surface wound, generally takes place when grooming, girthing-up or feeding are in operation. So too does biting but it is a more serious affair and can produce really ugly wounds. The thing to do is to rack-up the horse when grooming and feeding and trust to luck when girthing-up and of course whenever possible do the obvious thing by putting on a muzzle. All this is a great nuisance and rather than be bothered with it, many just endure what they assume can't be cured, and put up with the snatching and biting and content themselves with a bit of shouting at the first sign. This, by the way, is worse than useless.

Here is the cure which you can try with a lot of confidence—it requires time, patience, shouting is forbidden, and it's just as well to wear a pair of leather gloves. When grooming or girthing-up, every time the horse gives the familiar swing round of the head to bite, just push it back, and just keep on doing that, gently and firmly without word or reproach and without reward, for this would be associated with the swinging round of the head to bite. Obviously this can be done at other times than grooming and saddling, by just standing against the horse's side. You must just tire him out and make him see the futility of turning his head to bite which only results in its being pushed back again. It's as simple as that and is just a common sense cure which I thought out long ago.

A PERSONAL WORD FROM MELVIN POWERS
PUBLISHER, WILSHIRE BOOK COMPANY

Dear Friend:

My goal is to publish interesting, informative, and in-spirational books. You can help me accomplish this by answering the following questions, either by phone or by mail. Or, if convenient for you, I would welcome the oppor-tunity to visit with you in my office and hear your com-ments in person.

Did you enjoy reading this book? Why?

Would you enjoy reading another similar book?

What idea in the book impressed you the most?

If applicable to your situation, have you incorporated this idea in your daily life?

Is there a chapter that could serve as a theme for an entire book? Please explain.

If you have an idea for a book, I would welcome dis-cussing it with you. If you already have one in progress, write or call me concerning possible publication. I can be reached at (213) 875-1711 or (818) 983-1105.

Sincerely yours,

MELVIN POWERS

12015 Sherman Road
North Hollywood, California 91605

MELVIN POWERS SELF-IMPROVEMENT LIBRARY

ASTROLOGY
____ ASTROLOGY: HOW TO CHART YOUR HOROSCOPE *Max Heindel*   5.00
____ ASTROLOGY AND SEXUAL ANALYSIS *Morris C. Goodman*   5.00
____ ASTROLOGY MADE EASY *Astarte*   3.00
____ ASTROLOGY MADE PRACTICAL *Alexandra Kayhle*   3.00
____ ASTROLOGY, ROMANCE, YOU AND THE STARS *Anthony Norvell*   5.00
____ MY WORLD OF ASTROLOGY *Sydney Omarr*   7.00
____ THOUGHT DIAL *Sydney Omarr*   4.00
____ WHAT THE STARS REVEAL ABOUT THE MEN IN YOUR LIFE *Thelma White*   3.00

BRIDGE
____ BRIDGE BIDDING MADE EASY *Edwin B. Kantar*   10.00
____ BRIDGE CONVENTIONS *Edwin B. Kantar*   7.00
____ BRIDGE HUMOR *Edwin B. Kantar*   5.00
____ COMPETITIVE BIDDING IN MODERN BRIDGE *Edgar Kaplan*   7.00
____ DEFENSIVE BRIDGE PLAY COMPLETE *Edwin B. Kantar*   15.00
____ GAMESMAN BRIDGE — Play Better with Kantar *Edwin B. Kantar*   5.00
____ HOW TO IMPROVE YOUR BRIDGE *Alfred Sheinwold*   5.00
____ IMPROVING YOUR BIDDING SKILLS *Edwin B. Kantar*   4.00
____ INTRODUCTION TO DECLARER'S PLAY *Edwin B. Kantar*   5.00
____ INTRODUCTION TO DEFENDER'S PLAY *Edwin B. Kantar*   3.00
____ KANTAR FOR THE DEFENSE *Edwin B. Kantar*   7.00
____ KANTAR FOR THE DEFENSE VOLUME 2 *Edwin B. Kantar*   7.00
____ SHORT CUT TO WINNING BRIDGE *Alfred Sheinwold*   3.00
____ TEST YOUR BRIDGE PLAY *Edwin B. Kantar*   5.00
____ VOLUME 2 — TEST YOUR BRIDGE PLAY *Edwin B. Kantar*   5.00
____ WINNING DECLARER PLAY *Dorothy Hayden Truscott*   5.00

BUSINESS, STUDY & REFERENCE
____ CONVERSATION MADE EASY *Elliot Russell*   4.00
____ EXAM SECRET *Dennis B. Jackson*   3.00
____ FIX-IT BOOK *Arthur Symons*   2.00
____ HOW TO DEVELOP A BETTER SPEAKING VOICE *M. Hellier*   4.00
____ HOW TO SELF-PUBLISH YOUR BOOK & MAKE IT A BEST SELLER *Melvin Powers*   10.00
____ INCREASE YOUR LEARNING POWER *Geoffrey A. Dudley*   3.00
____ PRACTICAL GUIDE TO BETTER CONCENTRATION *Melvin Powers*   3.00
____ PRACTICAL GUIDE TO PUBLIC SPEAKING *Maurice Forley*   5.00
____ 7 DAYS TO FASTER READING *William S. Schaill*   5.00
____ SONGWRITERS' RHYMING DICTIONARY *Jane Shaw Whitfield*   7.00
____ SPELLING MADE EASY *Lester D. Basch & Dr. Milton Finkelstein*   3.00
____ STUDENT'S GUIDE TO BETTER GRADES *J. A. Rickard*   3.00
____ TEST YOURSELF — Find Your Hidden Talent *Jack Shafer*   3.00
____ YOUR WILL & WHAT TO DO ABOUT IT *Attorney Samuel G. Kling*   5.00

CALLIGRAPHY
____ ADVANCED CALLIGRAPHY *Katherine Jeffares*   7.00
____ CALLIGRAPHER'S REFERENCE BOOK *Anne Leptich & Jacque Evans*   7.00
____ CALLIGRAPHY — The Art of Beautiful Writing *Katherine Jeffares*   7.00
____ CALLIGRAPHY FOR FUN & PROFIT *Anne Leptich & Jacque Evans*   7.00
____ CALLIGRAPHY MADE EASY *Tina Serafini*   7.00

CHESS & CHECKERS
____ BEGINNER'S GUIDE TO WINNING CHESS *Fred Reinfeld*   5.00
____ CHESS IN TEN EASY LESSONS *Larry Evans*   5.00
____ CHESS MADE EASY *Milton L. Hanauer*   3.00
____ CHESS PROBLEMS FOR BEGINNERS *edited by Fred Reinfeld*   2.00
____ CHESS SECRETS REVEALED *Fred Reinfeld*   2.00
____ CHESS TACTICS FOR BEGINNERS *edited by Fred Reinfeld*   5.00
____ CHESS THEORY & PRACTICE *Morry & Mitchell*   2.00
____ HOW TO WIN AT CHECKERS *Fred Reinfeld*   3.00
____ 1001 BRILLIANT WAYS TO CHECKMATE *Fred Reinfeld*   5.00
____ 1001 WINNING CHESS SACRIFICES & COMBINATIONS *Fred Reinfeld*   5.00
____ SOVIET CHESS *Edited by R. G. Wade*   3.00

COOKERY & HERBS

____	CULPEPER'S HERBAL REMEDIES *Dr. Nicholas Culpeper*	3.00
____	FAST GOURMET COOKBOOK *Poppy Cannon*	2.50
____	GINSENG The Myth & The Truth *Joseph P. Hou*	3.00
____	HEALING POWER OF HERBS *May Bethel*	4.00
____	HEALING POWER OF NATURAL FOODS *May Bethel*	5.00
____	HERB HANDBOOK *Dawn MacLeod*	3.00
____	HERBS FOR HEALTH — How to Grow & Use Them *Louise Evans Doole*	4.00
____	HOME GARDEN COOKBOOK — Delicious Natural Food Recipes *Ken Kraft*	3.00
____	MEDICAL HERBALIST *edited by Dr. J. R. Yemm*	3.00
____	VEGETABLE GARDENING FOR BEGINNERS *Hugh Wiberg*	2.00
____	VEGETABLES FOR TODAY'S GARDENS *R. Milton Carleton*	2.00
____	VEGETARIAN COOKERY *Janet Walker*	4.00
____	VEGETARIAN COOKING MADE EASY & DELECTABLE *Veronica Vezza*	3.00
____	VEGETARIAN DELIGHTS — A Happy Cookbook for Health *K. R. Mehta*	2.00
____	VEGETARIAN GOURMET COOKBOOK *Joyce McKinnel*	3.00

GAMBLING & POKER

____	ADVANCED POKER STRATEGY & WINNING PLAY *A. D. Livingston*	5.00
____	HOW TO WIN AT DICE GAMES *Skip Frey*	3.00
____	HOW TO WIN AT POKER *Terence Reese & Anthony T. Watkins*	5.00
____	WINNING AT CRAPS *Dr. Lloyd T. Commins*	4.00
____	WINNING AT GIN *Chester Wander & Cy Rice*	3.00
____	WINNING AT POKER — An Expert's Guide *John Archer*	5.00
____	WINNING AT 21 — An Expert's Guide *John Archer*	5.00
____	WINNING POKER SYSTEMS *Norman Zadeh*	3.00

HEALTH

____	BEE POLLEN *Lynda Lyngheim & Jack Scagnetti*	3.00
____	DR. LINDNER'S SPECIAL WEIGHT CONTROL METHOD *P. G. Lindner, M.D.*	2.00
____	HELP YOURSELF TO BETTER SIGHT *Margaret Darst Corbett*	3.00
____	HOW TO IMPROVE YOUR VISION *Dr. Robert A. Kraskin*	3.00
____	HOW YOU CAN STOP SMOKING PERMANENTLY *Ernest Caldwell*	3.00
____	MIND OVER PLATTER *Peter G. Lindner, M.D.*	3.00
____	NATURE'S WAY TO NUTRITION & VIBRANT HEALTH *Robert J. Scrutton*	3.00
____	NEW CARBOHYDRATE DIET COUNTER *Patti Lopez-Pereira*	2.00
____	QUICK & EASY EXERCISES FOR FACIAL BEAUTY *Judy Smith-deal*	2.00
____	QUICK & EASY EXERCISES FOR FIGURE BEAUTY *Judy Smith-deal*	2.00
____	REFLEXOLOGY *Dr. Maybelle Segal*	4.00
____	REFLEXOLOGY FOR GOOD HEALTH *Anna Kaye & Don C. Matchan*	5.00
____	30 DAYS TO BEAUTIFUL LEGS *Dr. Marc Selner*	3.00
____	YOU CAN LEARN TO RELAX *Dr. Samuel Gutwirth*	3.00
____	YOUR ALLERGY — What To Do About It *Allan Knight, M.D.*	3.00

HOBBIES

____	BEACHCOMBING FOR BEGINNERS *Norman Hickin*	2.00
____	BLACKSTONE'S MODERN CARD TRICKS *Harry Blackstone*	3.00
____	BLACKSTONE'S SECRETS OF MAGIC *Harry Blackstone*	3.00
____	COIN COLLECTING FOR BEGINNERS *Burton Hobson & Fred Reinfeld*	5.00
____	ENTERTAINING WITH ESP *Tony 'Doc' Shiels*	2.00
____	400 FASCINATING MAGIC TRICKS YOU CAN DO *Howard Thurston*	4.00
____	HOW I TURN JUNK INTO FUN AND PROFIT *Sari*	3.00
____	HOW TO WRITE A HIT SONG & SELL IT *Tommy Boyce*	7.00
____	JUGGLING MADE EASY *Rudolf Dittrich*	3.00
____	MAGIC FOR ALL AGES *Walter Gibson*	4.00
____	MAGIC MADE EASY *Byron Wels*	2.00
____	STAMP COLLECTING FOR BEGINNERS *Burton Hobson*	3.00

HORSE PLAYERS' WINNING GUIDES

____	BETTING HORSES TO WIN *Les Conklin*	5.00
____	ELIMINATE THE LOSERS *Bob McKnight*	3.00
____	HOW TO PICK WINNING HORSES *Bob McKnight*	5.00
____	HOW TO WIN AT THE RACES *Sam (The Genius) Lewin*	5.00
____	HOW YOU CAN BEAT THE RACES *Jack Kavanagh*	5.00
____	MAKING MONEY AT THE RACES *David Barr*	5.00

_____ PAYDAY AT THE RACES *Les Conklin* 5.00
_____ SMART HANDICAPPING MADE EASY *William Bauman* 5.00
_____ SUCCESS AT THE HARNESS RACES *Barry Meadow* 5.00
_____ WINNING AT THE HARNESS RACES — An Expert's Guide *Nick Cammarano* 5.00

HUMOR

_____ HOW TO FLATTEN YOUR TUSH *Coach Marge Reardon* 2.00
_____ HOW TO MAKE LOVE TO YOURSELF *Ron Stevens & Joy Grdnic* 3.00
_____ JOKE TELLER'S HANDBOOK *Bob Orben* 5.00
_____ JOKES FOR ALL OCCASIONS *Al Schock* 5.00
_____ 2000 NEW LAUGHS FOR SPEAKERS *Bob Orben* 5.00
_____ 2,500 JOKES TO START 'EM LAUGHING *Bob Orben* 5.00

HYPNOTISM

_____ ADVANCED TECHNIQUES OF HYPNOSIS *Melvin Powers* 3.00
_____ BRAINWASHING AND THE CULTS *Paul A. Verdier, Ph.D.* 3.00
_____ CHILDBIRTH WITH HYPNOSIS *William S. Kroger, M.D.* 5.00
_____ HOW TO SOLVE Your Sex Problems with Self-Hypnosis *Frank S. Caprio, M.D.* 5.00
_____ HOW TO STOP SMOKING THRU SELF-HYPNOSIS *Leslie M. LeCron* 3.00
_____ HOW TO USE AUTO-SUGGESTION EFFECTIVELY *John Duckworth* 3.00
_____ HOW YOU CAN BOWL BETTER USING SELF-HYPNOSIS *Jack Heise* 4.00
_____ HOW YOU CAN PLAY BETTER GOLF USING SELF-HYPNOSIS *Jack Heise* 3.00
_____ HYPNOSIS AND SELF-HYPNOSIS *Bernard Hollander, M.D.* 5.00
_____ HYPNOTISM *(Originally published in 1893) Carl Sextus* 5.00
_____ HYPNOTISM & PSYCHIC PHENOMENA *Simeon Edmunds* 4.00
_____ HYPNOTISM MADE EASY *Dr. Ralph Winn* 3.00
_____ HYPNOTISM MADE PRACTICAL *Louis Orton* 5.00
_____ HYPNOTISM REVEALED *Melvin Powers* 3.00
_____ HYPNOTISM TODAY *Leslie LeCron and Jean Bordeaux, Ph.D.* 5.00
_____ MODERN HYPNOSIS *Lesley Kuhn & Salvatore Russo, Ph.D.* 5.00
_____ NEW CONCEPTS OF HYPNOSIS *Bernard C. Gindes, M.D.* 7.00
_____ NEW SELF-HYPNOSIS *Paul Adams* 5.00
_____ POST-HYPNOTIC INSTRUCTIONS — Suggestions for Therapy *Arnold Furst* 5.00
_____ PRACTICAL GUIDE TO SELF-HYPNOSIS *Melvin Powers* 3.00
_____ PRACTICAL HYPNOTISM *Philip Magonet, M.D.* 3.00
_____ SECRETS OF HYPNOTISM *S. J. Van Pelt, M.D.* 5.00
_____ SELF-HYPNOSIS A Conditioned-Response Technique *Laurence Sparks* 7.00
_____ SELF-HYPNOSIS Its Theory, Technique & Application *Melvin Powers* 3.00
_____ THERAPY THROUGH HYPNOSIS *edited by Raphael H. Rhodes* 5.00

JUDAICA

_____ MODERN ISRAEL *Lily Edelman* 2.00
_____ SERVICE OF THE HEART *Evelyn Garfiel, Ph.D.* 7.00
_____ STORY OF ISRAEL IN COINS *Jean & Maurice Gould* 2.00
_____ STORY OF ISRAEL IN STAMPS *Maxim & Gabriel Shamir* 1.00
_____ TONGUE OF THE PROPHETS *Robert St. John* 7.00

JUST FOR WOMEN

_____ COSMOPOLITAN'S GUIDE TO MARVELOUS MEN Fwd. by *Helen Gurley Brown* 3.00
_____ COSMOPOLITAN'S HANG-UP HANDBOOK Foreword by *Helen Gurley Brown* 4.00
_____ COSMOPOLITAN'S LOVE BOOK — A Guide to Ecstasy in Bed 7.00
_____ COSMOPOLITAN'S NEW ETIQUETTE GUIDE Fwd. by *Helen Gurley Brown* 4.00
_____ I AM A COMPLEAT WOMAN *Doris Hagopian & Karen O'Connor Sweeney* 3.00
_____ JUST FOR WOMEN — A Guide to the Female Body *Richard E. Sand, M.D.* 5.00
_____ NEW APPROACHES TO SEX IN MARRIAGE *John E. Eichenlaub, M.D.* 3.00
_____ SEXUALLY ADEQUATE FEMALE *Frank S. Caprio, M.D.* 3.00
_____ SEXUALLY FULFILLED WOMAN *Dr. Rachel Copelan* 5.00
_____ YOUR FIRST YEAR OF MARRIAGE *Dr. Tom McGinnis* 3.00

MARRIAGE, SEX & PARENTHOOD

_____ ABILITY TO LOVE *Dr. Allan Fromme* 6.00
_____ GUIDE TO SUCCESSFUL MARRIAGE *Drs. Albert Ellis & Robert Harper* 5.00
_____ HOW TO RAISE AN EMOTIONALLY HEALTHY, HAPPY CHILD *A. Ellis* 5.00
_____ SEX WITHOUT GUILT *Albert Ellis, Ph.D.* 5.00
_____ SEXUALLY ADEQUATE MALE *Frank S. Caprio, M.D.* 3.00

_____	SEXUALLY FULFILLED MAN *Dr. Rachel Copelan*	5.00
_____	STAYING IN LOVE *Dr. Norton F. Kristy*	7.00

MELVIN POWERS' MAIL ORDER LIBRARY

_____	HOW TO GET RICH IN MAIL ORDER *Melvin Powers*	15.00
_____	HOW TO WRITE A GOOD ADVERTISEMENT *Victor O. Schwab*	20.00
_____	MAIL ORDER MADE EASY *J. Frank Brumbaugh*	20.00
_____	U.S. MAIL ORDER SHOPPER'S GUIDE *Susan Spitzer*	10.00

METAPHYSICS & OCCULT

_____	BOOK OF TALISMANS, AMULETS & ZODIACAL GEMS *William Pavitt*	7.00
_____	CONCENTRATION — A Guide to Mental Mastery *Mouni Sadhu*	5.00
_____	CRITIQUES OF GOD *Edited by Peter Angeles*	7.00
_____	EXTRA-TERRESTRIAL INTELLIGENCE — The First Encounter	6.00
_____	FORTUNE TELLING WITH CARDS *P. Foli*	5.00
_____	HANDWRITING TELLS *Nadya Olyanova*	7.00
_____	HOW TO INTERPRET DREAMS, OMENS & FORTUNE TELLING SIGNS *Gettings*	5.00
_____	HOW TO UNDERSTAND YOUR DREAMS *Geoffrey A. Dudley*	3.00
_____	ILLUSTRATED YOGA *William Zorn*	3.00
_____	IN DAYS OF GREAT PEACE *Mouni Sadhu*	3.00
_____	LSD — THE AGE OF MIND *Bernard Roseman*	2.00
_____	MAGICIAN — His Training and Work *W. E. Butler*	3.00
_____	MEDITATION *Mouni Sadhu*	7.00
_____	MODERN NUMEROLOGY *Morris C. Goodman*	5.00
_____	NUMEROLOGY — ITS FACTS AND SECRETS *Ariel Yvon Taylor*	3.00
_____	NUMEROLOGY MADE EASY *W. Mykian*	5.00
_____	PALMISTRY MADE EASY *Fred Gettings*	5.00
_____	PALMISTRY MADE PRACTICAL *Elizabeth Daniels Squire*	5.00
_____	PALMISTRY SECRETS REVEALED *Henry Frith*	4.00
_____	PROPHECY IN OUR TIME *Martin Ebon*	2.50
_____	SUPERSTITION — Are You Superstitious? *Eric Maple*	2.00
_____	TAROT *Mouni Sadhu*	8.00
_____	TAROT OF THE BOHEMIANS *Papus*	7.00
_____	WAYS TO SELF-REALIZATION *Mouni Sadhu*	3.00
_____	WITCHCRAFT, MAGIC & OCCULTISM — A Fascinating History *W. B. Crow*	5.00
_____	WITCHCRAFT — THE SIXTH SENSE *Justine Glass*	7.00
_____	WORLD OF PSYCHIC RESEARCH *Hereward Carrington*	2.00

SELF-HELP & INSPIRATIONAL

_____	CHARISMA How You Can Have That "Special Magic" *Marcia Grad*	7.00
_____	DAILY POWER FOR JOYFUL LIVING *Dr. Donald Curtis*	5.00
_____	DYNAMIC THINKING *Melvin Powers*	5.00
_____	GREATEST POWER IN THE UNIVERSE *U. S. Andersen*	5.00
_____	GROW RICH WHILE YOU SLEEP *Ben Sweetland*	7.00
_____	GROWTH THROUGH REASON *Albert Ellis, Ph.D.*	7.00
_____	GUIDE TO PERSONAL HAPPINESS *Albert Ellis, Ph.D. & Irving Becker, Ed. D.*	5.00
_____	HANDWRITING ANALYSIS MADE EASY *John Marley*	5.00
_____	HELPING YOURSELF WITH APPLIED PSYCHOLOGY *R. Henderson*	2.00
_____	HOW TO ATTRACT GOOD LUCK *A. H. Z. Carr*	5.00
_____	HOW TO BE GREAT *Dr. Donald Curtis*	5.00
_____	HOW TO DEVELOP A WINNING PERSONALITY *Martin Panzer*	5.00
_____	HOW TO DEVELOP AN EXCEPTIONAL MEMORY *Young & Gibson*	5.00
_____	HOW TO LIVE WITH A NEUROTIC *Albert Ellis, Ph. D.*	5.00
_____	HOW TO OVERCOME YOUR FEARS *M. P. Leahy, M.D.*	3.00
_____	HOW TO SUCCEED *Brian Adams*	7.00
_____	HUMAN PROBLEMS & HOW TO SOLVE THEM *Dr. Donald Curtis*	5.00
_____	I CAN *Ben Sweetland*	7.00
_____	I WILL *Ben Sweetland*	3.00
_____	LEFT-HANDED PEOPLE *Michael Barsley*	5.00
_____	MAGIC IN YOUR MIND *U. S. Andersen*	7.00
_____	MAGIC OF THINKING BIG *Dr. David J. Schwartz*	3.00
_____	MAGIC POWER OF YOUR MIND *Walter M. Germain*	7.00
_____	MENTAL POWER THROUGH SLEEP SUGGESTION *Melvin Powers*	3.00

___	NEVER UNDERESTIMATE THE SELLING POWER OF A WOMAN *Dottie Walters*	7.00
___	NEW GUIDE TO RATIONAL LIVING *Albert Ellis, Ph.D. & R. Harper, Ph.D.*	3.00
___	PROJECT YOU *A Manual of Rational Assertiveness Training Paris & Casey*	6.00
___	PSYCHO-CYBERNETICS *Maxwell Maltz, M.D.*	5.00
___	PSYCHOLOGY OF HANDWRITING *Nadya Olyanova*	7.00
___	SALES CYBERNETICS *Brian Adams*	7.00
___	SCIENCE OF MIND IN DAILY LIVING *Dr. Donald Curtis*	5.00
___	SECRET OF SECRETS *U. S. Andersen*	7.00
___	SECRET POWER OF THE PYRAMIDS *U. S. Andersen*	7.00
___	SELF-THERAPY FOR THE STUTTERER *Malcolm Frazer*	3.00
___	STUTTERING AND WHAT YOU CAN DO ABOUT IT *W. Johnson, Ph.D.*	2.50
___	SUCCESS-CYBERNETICS *U. S. Andersen*	6.00
___	10 DAYS TO A GREAT NEW LIFE *William E. Edwards*	3.00
___	THINK AND GROW RICH *Napoleon Hill*	5.00
___	THINK YOUR WAY TO SUCCESS *Dr. Lew Losoncy*	5.00
___	THREE MAGIC WORDS *U. S. Andersen*	7.00
___	TREASURY OF COMFORT *edited by Rabbi Sidney Greenberg*	5.00
___	TREASURY OF THE ART OF LIVING *Sidney S. Greenberg*	5.00
___	WHAT YOUR HANDWRITING REVEALS *Albert E. Hughes*	3.00
___	YOU ARE NOT THE TARGET *Laura Huxley*	5.00
___	YOUR SUBCONSCIOUS POWER *Charles M. Simmons*	7.00
___	YOUR THOUGHTS CAN CHANGE YOUR LIFE *Dr. Donald Curtis*	5.00

SPORTS

___	BICYCLING FOR FUN AND GOOD HEALTH *Kenneth E. Luther*	2.00
___	BILLIARDS — Pocket • Carom • Three Cushion *Clive Cottingham, Jr.*	5.00
___	CAMPING-OUT 101 Ideas & Activities *Bruno Knobel*	2.00
___	COMPLETE GUIDE TO FISHING *Vlad Evanoff*	2.00
___	HOW TO IMPROVE YOUR RACQUETBALL *Lubarsky Kaufman & Scagnetti*	5.00
___	HOW TO WIN AT POCKET BILLIARDS *Edward D. Knuchell*	5.00
___	JOY OF WALKING *Jack Scagnetti*	3.00
___	LEARNING & TEACHING SOCCER SKILLS *Eric Worthington*	3.00
___	MOTORCYCLING FOR BEGINNERS *I. G. Edmonds*	3.00
___	RACQUETBALL FOR WOMEN *Toni Hudson, Jack Scagnetti & Vince Rondone*	3.00
___	RACQUETBALL MADE EASY *Steve Lubarsky, Rod Delson & Jack Scagnetti*	5.00
___	SECRET OF BOWLING STRIKES *Dawson Taylor*	5.00
___	SECRET OF PERFECT PUTTING *Horton Smith & Dawson Taylor*	5.00
___	SOCCER — The Game & How to Play It *Gary Rosenthal*	5.00
___	STARTING SOCCER *Edward F. Dolan, Jr.*	3.00

TENNIS LOVERS' LIBRARY

___	BEGINNER'S GUIDE TO WINNING TENNIS *Helen Hull Jacobs*	2.00
___	HOW TO BEAT BETTER TENNIS PLAYERS *Loring Fiske*	4.00
___	HOW TO IMPROVE YOUR TENNIS — Style, Strategy & Analysis *C. Wilson*	2.00
___	PLAY TENNIS WITH ROSEWALL *Ken Rosewall*	2.00
___	PSYCH YOURSELF TO BETTER TENNIS *Dr. Walter A. Luszki*	2.00
___	TENNIS FOR BEGINNERS, *Dr. H. A. Murray*	2.00
___	TENNIS MADE EASY *Joel Brecheen*	4.00
___	WEEKEND TENNIS — How to Have Fun & Win at the Same Time *Bill Talbert*	3.00
___	WINNING WITH PERCENTAGE TENNIS — Smart Strategy *Jack Lowe*	2.00

WILSHIRE PET LIBRARY

___	DOG OBEDIENCE TRAINING *Gust Kessopulos*	5.00
___	DOG TRAINING MADE EASY & FUN *John W. Kellogg*	4.00
___	HOW TO BRING UP YOUR PET DOG *Kurt Unkelbach*	2.00
___	HOW TO RAISE & TRAIN YOUR PUPPY *Jeff Griffen*	5.00
___	PIGEONS: HOW TO RAISE & TRAIN THEM *William H. Allen, Jr.*	2.00

*The books listed above can be obtained from your book dealer or directly from
Melvin Powers. When ordering, please remit $1.00 postage for the first book
and 50¢ for each additional book.*

Melvin Powers

12015 Sherman Road, No. Hollywood, California 91605

NOTES

NOTES